Praise for *Leaders as Teachers Action Guide*

"For a small business that has dreamed of creating a culture of learning or an in-house learning organization, this book is a must read! *Leaders as Teachers Action Guide* delivers a simple, practical, and cost effective blueprint of how to leverage your current talent and experience to grow leaders at all levels, enhance your culture, and drive people development. This book will propel you forward in your journey of being a successful and professionally managed organization."

Scott P. George
Director, Research and Product Development
Aileron

"*Leaders as Teachers Action Guide* is a practical and compelling guide to achieving impactful results for leaders serving as teachers and employees participating as learners. This is a great resource for leaders who want to shape a learning organization and high performance culture."

Shawn D. Zimmerman
Vice President, Global Talent and Organization Capability
The Hershey Company

"This is a great resource that goes well beyond insights on the value of a leaders-as-teachers initiative. It is a very practical guide that provides comprehensive instructions and guidance on how to implement a LAT program in any organization."

Neal R. Goodman, PhD
President, Global Dynamics, Inc.
Professor Emeritus, Saint Peter's University

"*Leaders as Teachers Action Guide* is a must read and practical roadmap for companies of any size to launch or strengthen a leaders-as-teachers program. The benefits are significant, with insights on many topics, including instilling leadership values and skills, strengthening organizational culture, and communication and driving business results."

Diana Oreck
Vice President
Ritz-Carlton Leadership Center

"This action guide provides myriad practical tools for building a leaders-as-teachers approach—from broad brush planning to detailed execution tactics, you will find opportunities to address your organization's unique situation."

Deb Tees, EdD
Director, Talent and Organizational Capability
At a Fortune 50 Aerospace and Defense Company

"*Leaders as Teachers Action Guide* is a highly valuable resource for use in organizational learning. By augmenting our formal curriculum with the use of real world applications, we've experienced increased employee engagement with greater content relevancy. Moreover, using Merck leaders as part of our faculty has also improved our employee and manager relationships, sparked new networks within the organization, and has proven to be very cost effective. We're fans!"

Nancy Singer, RPh
Executive Director, Enterprise Learning
Merck & Co., Inc.

"In my company, leaders as teachers has become a vital component of our change management plans. When our leaders teach, they demonstrate commitment and a deep understanding of where they want to take the organization. When our associates see our leaders teach, they gain an accelerated understanding of what is expected from them. This is how we build urgency and excitement for creating a more competitive, engaging, and vital organization."

Jerry Hurwitz
Senior Vice President, Human Resources
BD (Becton Dickinson)

"*Leaders as Teachers Action Guide* makes a strong case that as leaders we have a profound opportunity to coach our colleagues and impact our organization when we teach, and provides practical information to teach leaders to teach."

Craig D. Weidemann, PhD
Vice President, Outreach and Vice Provost for Online Education
The Pennsylvania State University

"In the learning and development profession, there are certain books that really standout in making a significant contribution to the depth and breadth of the profession. The *Leaders as Teachers Action Guide* is one of those books that is sure to set the standard for enabling practitioners to drive successful leadership development in their organizations."

J. Keith Dunbar
Director, Talent Management
Leidos

"*Leaders as Teachers Action Guide* is your hands-on-resource to building a LAT model in your organization. This engaging book is filled with the most up-to-date thinking, tools, insights, and best practices from top-notch companies. The authors, Ed, Lisa, and Sue, are credible thought leaders and have done a nice job modeling what they teach in this book. I highly recommend it!"

Diane Holman
Chief Talent Development Officer
Wolters Kluwer

"We're in the process of implementing a leaders-as-teachers program at Keurig Green Mountain and I can't wait to integrate all the highlights, notes, and follow-up actions from *Leaders as Teachers Action Guide*. Ed, Sue, and Lisa did a great job of creating a practical and leading-edge process for implementing LAT in companies and firms of all sizes and complexity."

Jayne Johnson
VP, Talent, Learning, and Organizational Development
Keurig Green Mountain, Inc.

"*Leaders as Teachers Action Guide* is sure to be a well-used resource for any organization focused on learning and development. Filled with easy-to-follow steps and tools, this practical resource is a must-have for those looking to more effectively leverage leadership in teaching roles."

Robin Renschen
Director, Learning and Development
McCarthy Building Companies, Inc.

"Five years ago, Ed Betof challenged organizations to unlock the teaching potential of their top talent by implementing a leaders-as-teachers program in his book, *Leaders as Teachers: Unlock the Teaching Potential of Your Company's Best and Brightest*. The authors packed this sequel with innovative case studies and organized them into a coherent framework of ready-to-use examples that can be applied in any organization."

Mary McNevin
Chief Learning Officer
Signature Healthcare

"The leaders-teachers methodology is a powerful catalyst to accelerate leadership development, strengthen culture, and ultimately drive business results. Ed, Lisa, and Sue offer a comprehensive, step-by-step approach that any organization can leverage to get started or take their development activities to the next level."

Heidi Capozzi
VP, Leadership Talent Management and Organization Effectiveness
Boeing

"*Leaders as Teachers Action Guide* practices what it teaches! This book provides proven, powerful payoffs for individual leaders and their organizations. This insightful guide is filled with terrific, time-tested teaching and training tips that will help readers to lead and teach with ease. You'll see that enlightening will strike more than once in this actionable gold mine."

Joel Goodman, EdD
Founder and Director
The HUMOR Project, Inc.

LEADERS
AS
TEACHERS
ACTION GUIDE

Proven Approaches for Unlocking
Success in Your Organization

Edward Betof • Lisa M.D. Owens • Sue Todd

ASTD Press is an internationally renowned source of insightful and practical information on workplace learning, performance, and professional development.

ASTD Press
1640 King Street Box 1443
Alexandria, VA 22313-1443 USA

Ordering information: Books published by ASTD Press can be purchased by visiting ASTD's website at store.astd.org or by calling 800.628.2783 or 703.683.8100.

Library of Congress Control Number: 2014934633

ISBN-10: 1-56286-919-1
ISBN: 978-1-56286-919-9
e-ISBN: 978-1-60728-406-2

ASTD Press Editorial Staff:
Director: Glenn Saltzman
Manager and Editor, ASTD Press: Ashley McDonald
Associate Editor: Sarah Cough
Community of Practice Manager, Human Capital: Ann Parker
Editorial Assistant: Ashley Slade
Cover Design: Marisa Kelly
Interior Design: Bey Bello
Interior Production: Abella Publishing Services, LLC
Printed by Versa Press, Inc., East Peoria, IL, www.versapress.com

Dedications

To my wife and life partner, Nila, with whom I have shared love and family and from whom I have learned life and leadership lessons for more than 45 years. And to our adult children, Ari, Allison, and daughter-in law, Shauna, who model everyday what it means to be leader-teachers in their professional and family lives.

To my late Mom and Dad, Jean and Martin Betof, who taught me essential lessons throughout their lives and when I needed roots and wings the most.

To Sidney B. Simon and Leland Howe, professors who inspired me to be a leader-teacher during my undergraduate and graduate school programs. To Herb Conrad (The Coach) and to Ed Ludwig who in their own ways each set the "tone at the top" at Roche Pharmaceuticals and BD respectively, thereby empowering my career and contributions in ways I could have only imagined earlier in my life.

—Ed Betof

■ ■ ■

To my husband, Richard, of 35 years, whose ongoing, daily support made this book possible.

To my mother, Pastor Dee Donnelly, who was my first editor.

To John Waldman, retired P&G executive, who gave me one of my first keys to unlocking success as I began coaching leader-teachers. After having provided John with a personal assessment of his training capabilities, he said to me, "Thank you for telling me what I was doing right. I've always been told I was good at teaching, but, to be honest, I was guessing about what to do. I was just doing whatever felt right. Now I know what I am doing right, because you told me. So now I will do more of those things, and will do them with confidence." Thanks for the key, John.

—Lisa M.D. Owens

■ ■ ■

For God and my whole doggone family:

    The Ms—Mom, Maggie, Miki, Maisie, Maddi, Margo

    The A—Alan

    The Bs—Bob, Becky, Brooks

    The D—Dad

    The Js—Jack, Jackie

    The Rs—Rodney, Rodney

    The Ss—Sadie, and Spencer

—Sue Todd

Contents

Foreword

■ ■ ■

"Great idea boss . . . you go first."

Have you ever been in a really good learning event when someone challenges the proceedings by telling the organizers that they got the invitations wrong? The remark usually falls along the lines of acknowledging the value of the course content, but that it needs to be taught to the boss or "those other people" first. In other words, "I can't really put this into practice until my boss goes first."

Surprisingly later in my career, as I sit in management meetings I hear a similar complaint. A senior leader will say, "This organization would work so much better if only employees would act differently." In other words, "great idea employee, you go first."

After those comments, we are stuck, taking a mindset that those outside the room own the obligation to improve. And that's where a leaders-as-teachers practice becomes the enabler to get unstuck and move-forward. With leaders in the room, and leaders actively teaching and role modeling, we can all have great ideas and act together.

I've been fortunate to be witness to many such move forward moments in my career.

Awhile back, I invited Steve, my company's CEO, to kick off a new manager training class. He proceeded to amaze everyone by previewing one of the course topics. "This is an important program for you and the company, but I have to warn you that the trainers are going to make you read your leadership 360 report," he said. "While the feedback isn't always pleasant, I've found it valuable."

Steve then proceeded to share highlights of his most recent 360 report, quickly noting his high scores and strengths, but then transitioning to a low score. "My team is telling me they want more feedback from me," he said. "And while I thought I was doing enough, it's important for me, as their boss, to provide the coaching they need." Steve went on to tell a story of how a former boss had shared an observation of him that was insightful and a defining growth moment in his career.

With that opening session from the CEO, the remainder of the program was magical and reminded me of the power of leaders-as-teachers. By being in the room and serving as an active guide, Steve demonstrated:

- No leader is perfect, not even the CEO. Leaders must have the humility and confidence to be authentic and transparent.
- It's smart to be open, to know yourself better, and to strive to improve throughout your career. If you are an effective leader, learning is always on your agenda.
- Part of the leader's job is to teach and raise-up other leaders.

Steve would return to open classes on a regular basis and share his feedback story until one day he did something different. His introduction was the same but this time he added that a new 360 report gave him much higher marks on providing feedback. With a grin he added, "The comments informed me that my employees saw the progress and remarked that they were now getting plenty of feedback so no need to do more! So now I'm working on something else." And as everyone chuckled at the remark, I added one more item to what he did well as a teaching leader:

- As you teach, keep it all in perspective and don't take yourself too seriously.

All in all, Steve was a great asset to have in learning venues, and I wish it had been that easy with others I invited into the room to be a teaching leader. In fact, a leaders-as-teachers approach can be hard work for all concerned. It is likely you could experience more of the downside of this approach than its benefits. The "why to do it" may be compelling, but the "how to do it well" is equally important but less known.

That's where this book comes in handy. The authors have a remarkable track record of success bringing this approach to life for a variety of organizations. Ed, Lisa, and Sue have been there before and serve as wise guides along the way to the reader. More impressively, they have reached out to a wide spectrum of organizations and practitioners, compiling the most comprehensive toolkit in the field. Finally, the structure of the book is engaging and practical, filled with worksheets, quick tips, and illustrative case studies.

As you dig into this book, imagine Lisa, Ed, and Sue at your side as your personal teaching leaders. They can provide the wisdom and encouragement you need as you engage your leaders to become teachers. My hope is that as they join you in the classroom, your leaders will emulate Steve's inspirational style, demonstrating:

Here's a good idea, let's all learn it together!

—Kevin D. Wilde
VP, Organization Effectiveness & Chief Learning Officer
General Mills
Author, *Dancing With the Talent Stars: 25 Moves That Matter Now*
October 2013

Acknowledgments

We wish to express our thanks to the following individuals, without whom this book would not be possible. This book includes, not only our own experiences with the leaders-as-teachers approach, but also the many insights and stories from a wide range of people and companies. Thank you to all of you who have contributed.

Thank you to the following people who spent time with us in interviews: Ann Schulte, Brian Parker, Charlotte Otto, Deb Wijnberg, Douglas Clayton, Jerry Lewis, John Leikhim, John Messman, Kevin D. Wilde, Mark Bocianski, Michael Abrams, Mike Kelly, Nancy Allen, Ricky Mathews, Sharon Moshayof, and Sheri Peterson.

Thanks, too, to those who were gracious enough to allow us to quote them; who responded to our survey questions; or provided us with materials, insights, comments, or assistance for this book, including: Amy Bastuga, Ari Katanick, Arlette Watwood, Beth Carlson, Bob R. Sanders, Bruce Stanley, Carra Simmons, Chris Kreuser, Christine Nester, Daniel Coombes, David Learmond, Dennis Hirotsu, Douglas Holt, (Jacob) Eli Thomas, Eliska Meyers, Gavin Galloway, Glenda Valero de Silano, Jay Glasscock, Jay Johnson, Jean Ibrahim, Jennifer Pope-Moore, Jerry Hurwitz, Joe Steier, Jonathan Wilson, Kate Maurin, Kathy Broxterman, Kelly Muno, Ken Edelman, Kirsten Hawley, Lauri Harwood, Linda Michalopoulos, Mary McNevin, Nancy Peltz, Noreen Coleman, Patrick Schnabel, Ray Takagiku, Rebecca Ray, Robert Sachs, Sharon Mitchell, Stephen Buchman, Stephen Sichak, Susan Armstrong, Teresa Roche, and William Kozy.

Special thanks to Kevin D. Wilde who drew from his years of experience at GE and General Mills. Kevin shared his perspectives on leaders as teachers with us and wrote a personalized and insightful foreword that perfectly set the tone for this book.

Thanks too to our editors, Ann Parker and Sarah Cough, who guided our writing of this book from its inception through its completion. Ann's and Sarah's insights, support, attention to detail, and flexibility in working with us are deeply appreciated. Ann and Sarah not only provided very useful ideas and feedback that sharpened our writing, but also remained open to our ideas and input throughout the writing of this book. For this and their commitment to excellence throughout the writing of this book, we are highly appreciative.

Introduction

Welcome to the *Leaders as Teachers Action Guide*. We wish you the best on your journey to inspire your leaders to serve as teachers. It is a strategy that has been proven to drive success for many companies and organizations.

We wrote this book to help you create or expand your own leaders-as-teachers (LAT) learning programs. In our experience, when we enable leaders to lead people through the process of learning and development, great things happen. We share this book with you in the hope that you will have similar experiences.

We see this book as the sequel to *Leaders as Teachers: Unlocking the Teaching Potential of Your Company's Best and Brightest*, yet it is also a book that stands on its own as a step-by-step guide. It shares not only our own in-depth experience with the topic, but also a wealth of experience from more than a dozen companies that we have interviewed and worked with.

This book is written primarily for the following readers:

- learning leaders, such as chief learning officers, vice presidents of talent development, and directors of leadership development
- members of learning, training, and development teams who will contribute to, and implement, the LAT vision and goals
- business and functional leaders who can selectively use ideas and methods in the book to help them be better leader-teachers and coaches on a daily basis, as well as in the classroom
- HR leaders, especially those responsible for strengthening the organization's leadership pipeline or cultivating an organization culture of teaching and learning
- past readers who have found value in the LAT book and desire more on the topic.

While this book is a step-by-step guide and starts at the beginning, we recognize that many of you are already well on your way with LAT programs. This book is designed to help you jump into the **leaders-as-teachers approach** at whatever point best matches your current situation, be it forming (Part I), designing (Part II), or executing and expanding (Part III). Don't worry about missing something; if it's critical, there will be specific references to earlier parts of the book to help you move forward quickly.

To start you on your journey, here are a few steps to help you use the book.

Step 1: Familiarize yourself with the chapter format. By understanding the layout and icons used in each chapter you can more quickly find what you want when you need it.

Step 2: Get an overview. Read the table of contents for a bird's-eye view, and the description at the beginning of each part to see one level down.

Step 3: Read the Foreword by Kevin D. Wilde. Kevin is the chief learning officer for General Mills, selected as CLO of the Year 2007, and formerly a learning leader at GE Crotonville.

Step 4: Scan the Terminology section in the Appendix to familiarize yourself with the meaning of words and phrases unique to LAT, such as **go to the light** and **unique leadership perspective**.

Step 5: Read the stories at the end for inspiration. Jump to the last chapter, from time to time, to read another LAT success story to keep you inspired on your journey.

We wish you great success and invite you to share your successes with us and others, using any social collaborative method in your toolkit. Together, we will all continue the learning journey.

Sincerely,

Ed, Lisa, and Sue

Chapter Format

Each chapter has a similar layout and icons to help you quickly find just what you want when you need it.

In Every Chapter

Each chapter starts with Find Your Answers and ends with Your Turn.

Find Your Answers

This short list of questions can help you focus on applying concepts in the chapter to your unique situation. These questions are reprised in Your Turn.

Your Turn

At the end of each chapter, this set of questions can assist you as you reflect and apply what you have been learning.

Throughout the Book

Throughout each chapter, watch for these icons for content that is the most relevant for you. These include:

Learn By Doing

Don't skip these! They are loaded with content, and are mini-examples of active teaching. These sections will help you apply what you are learning, and in doing so, deepen your understanding.

Learning From Leader-Teachers

provides a wealth of perspective and stories from leaders who are teachers.

Insights From Learning Professionals

shares stories, advice, and insights from leaders of learning organizations who have successfully guided leaders-as-teachers programs.

Science Notes

gives insight into relevant behavioral science and neuroscience research.

Quick Tips

are practical, simple hints, tips, and proven creative suggestions.

Framing a Leaders as Teachers Approach for Your Workplace

Part I guides you to structure your **leaders-as-teachers** (LAT) initiative at a high level using three steps: confirm *why* the LAT approach is right for today's business, choose *what* to build, and identify *who* should build it.

Chapter 1: Leaders as Teachers—Today's Imperative

Get grounded in the documentation and research demonstrating the benefits of the LAT approach for today's businesses. Weave this into your own LAT initiative proposals and discussions.

Chapter 2: Choose Your Starting Plan

Map out your LAT starting plan with considerations for business drivers, vision, scope, and how to build internal support. Select an initial structure for delivery and governance.

Chapter 3: Form Your LAT Team

It takes a team and leadership to achieve a successful LAT culture. Gather your team, lead them, and ultimately, grow them using **progression** plans.

Chapter 1

Leaders as Teachers— Today's Imperative

"The conductor doesn't make a sound. The power of the conductor is derived from making other people feel powerful."

—Ben Zander, conductor of the Boston Philharmonic and author of *The Art of Possibility*

■ ■ ■

 Find Your Answers

Increasingly, organizations are turning to a wide variety of leaders-as-teachers approaches. As you read, think about your answers to these questions:

- Which of the seven cornerstone LAT principles are relevant for your situation?
- Which of these elements will help you engage others in the LAT approach?
  - historical basis of leaders as teachers
  - evidence and experience
  - professional examples

More than ever the CEOs, boards, and executive teams of highly successful companies and organizations are focusing on their talent management, learning, and leadership development practices. The goal of these talent management and leadership development efforts is to ensure that engaged and effective leaders and professionals are in key roles now and in the future. A vital method adopted by many of these organizations is the practice of leaders developing leaders—serving as teachers, coaches, and mentors. How to best implement such a practice is the focus of this Action Guide.

The *Leaders as Teachers Action Guide* is based on seven cornerstone principles:

1. *One of the best ways to ensure top and bottom line growth is to continuously develop strong leaders and professionals.* Talent development and having a robust talent pipeline is an irrefutable winning strategy of best practice companies. These companies think and act on their top line, bottom line, and talent pipeline. Effective leadership is the best insurance for business success and sustainability. Besides the obvious advantages of having strong leaders versus poor or dysfunctional ones, stock market analysts place significant value on effective company leadership. Essentially, they reward effective leadership at a premium. Analysts also penalize companies for having ineffective leaders and leadership practices.

2. *The organizations that utilize a LAT approach provide themselves with a distinct competitive advantage.* The LAT approach:

   - helps to drive business results and company value
   - stimulates the learning and development of leaders and associates
   - improves the leadership perspective and skills of those who teach
   - strengthens the organizational culture and communications
   - promotes positive business and organizational change
   - reduces costs by leveraging top talent, especially when guided by skilled learning leaders and professionals.

3. *Exemplar companies are made up of leaders at many levels who teach very effectively in the moment, as well as in learning programs.* These leaders teach, coach, and often serve as mentors to others. Who better to be the role models and teach or co-teach the company's strategy, values, culture, and competency priorities? Top-notch development of talent is a key predictor of sustained

business success and operational excellence. "First who, then what" is one of the most instructive findings in Jim Collins's landmark *Good to Great* and *Great by Choice* research (Collins 2008; Collins and Hansen 2011). Leaders are those who show the way forward.

4. *The practice of leaders serving as teachers is a time-tested, centuries-old concept that has great relevance for today's organizations.* The long history of how experienced leaders teach, coach, and mentor others serves as a compass for us. Sharing the wisdom, perspectives, and values of those who have learned from experience can provide lessons that should not be lost by any organization. In a similar way, this guide has dozens of practical ideas, activities, and practices that come from what companies and organizations have learned during their LAT journey. These are companies we have studied, consulted, or worked in ourselves. Their business and functional **leader-teachers** and their learning leaders have generously shared their experiences with us so others can benefit.

5. *All organizations can implement a LAT approach in some shape, size, or form.* What is right for one company may not fit for another. Some organizations can go large-scale comparatively quickly, while other companies should take small and slow, incremental steps. The *Leaders as Teachers Action Guide* is written as a practical, hands-on resource. It is designed to help organizations, learning executives and professionals, and leaders at many levels to effectively implement or strengthen their LAT approach in a manner that will work in their organizations.

6. *Active or experiential teaching and learning is what makes the process come alive and have real impact.* There are many ways to avoid "death by PowerPoint syndrome." **Active teaching** not only improves learning and increases the likelihood of learning transfer, it makes teaching and facilitation enjoyable and a valued activity for leaders. As a result, leaders frequently ask to teach in future programs.

7. *Learning leaders and professionals have an essential role in the leader-teacher process.* They show the way. They are change agents necessary for the LAT approach to be successfully implemented. They frequently teach with leader-teachers and help them be the "stars." Learning leaders and professionals prepare leaders

in a wide variety of ways and serve as program designers and, sometimes, instructional technologists. This Action Guide is designed with learning leaders and professionals in mind. The model of concept to idea to application can be found throughout.

 # Learn By Doing: Historical Leaders

• Great philosophers such as Plato, Aristotle, and Socrates from the Golden Age of Greece	• Senior military and law enforcement personnel
• Elders, shamans, or medicine men from early native civilizations	• Contemporary business leaders in selected high-performance companies
• Leaders of the great religions over the centuries	• Great educators in elementary school through university
• Artisans or skilled craftsmen beginning in the middle ages	• Athletic and performance arts coaches
• Leaders of scouting groups such as Girl Scouts, Boy Scouts, and 4H	• Sage friends and trusted advisers
• Labor union craft masters and foremen	• Loving parents and grandparents
• Experienced physicians and nurses throughout the history of medical education	

What do the above individuals, groups, and professionals have in common?

_____

_____

The Historical Perspective

The common element for every person in the Learn By Doing activity is that they are examples of leaders who have served as teachers, coaches, and sometimes mentors. They have helped and guided others' development. They have taught important lessons, provided a brain to pick, an ear to listen, and sometimes a push in the right direction.

Leaders have served as teachers, coaches, and mentors for centuries in civilizations around the globe. Elders taught the basic means of survival, customs, and traditions to the young. The great religions passed their teachings from one generation to another. From these teachers, leaders emerged and continued the cycle of teaching, learning, surviving, and thriving.

This brief history lesson is a window into the importance, dynamics, and staying power of successful teaching experiences. It provides insight into several key characteristics of excellent leader-teachers and coaches. They share knowledge, experience, perspective, and counsel and are sensitive to others' needs and personalities. Commonly, this enables them to be viewed as positive role models. They are able to establish, build, and sustain supportive, trusting, and confidential relationships. In short, the best leader-teachers are trusted advisers who create opportunities for learning, growth, development, and positive change in others. The examples of individuals, groups, and professionals listed in the activity are models of these characteristics.

Now dial forward from the ancient civilizations to today's complex organizations with their need and inherent competition for talented leaders. Leaders who serve as teachers and coaches are vital organizational resources. They support the development of current and emerging professionals, managers, and executives. The use of leader-teachers can be a highly effective leadership development strategy.

Leader-teachers are highly valued in many contemporary businesses, government, educational, and human services organizations. However, despite the demonstrated and time-tested value of leaders serving as mentors and teachers, many organizations place themselves at a competitive and talent disadvantage by failing to utilize these developmental resources. These leaders are typically experienced, motivated, and highly engaged. Not making use of their experience and expertise can be a lost developmental opportunity for many organizations (Betof 2010).

Leaders as Teachers Examples

Throughout this Action Guide we will refer to many company and organizational practices. These range from teaching in executive and leadership programs to using social media to communicate and teach across large sectors of employees. Some companies such as GE, Honeywell, P&G, Boeing, 3M, and General Mills were early adopters. Other companies such as Banner Health and SES have more

💬 Insights From Learning Professionals

"I conducted a working session in January 2012, for the purposes of moving forward with the content for a strategy course, which our executives would facilitate. I set up a meeting with the CEO, his direct reports, and the key people who were creating the strategy plans. So there were at least a dozen executives in the room. I had all the PowerPoint slides for the course printed out on the wall and walked them through each slide. It soon became clear to the CEO and the chief development officer that the colleagues in the room were not completely aligned with various important elements of our company's strategic plan. This was partly due to acquisitions of several companies over the past few years. The course design became a catalyst for the internal alignment process. Over the next weeks, the CEO and executives met separately and worked through their differing points of view so that the new course would truly reflect the corporate strategy that all our executives were now pursuing. This is just one example of how the LAT approach provided a very substantial benefit to our business."

—Doug Clayton, Senior VP of HR, SES

recently leveraged their leaders in teaching roles and are just realizing the important benefits. BD not only utilizes their leaders around the world to teach in their corporate university, but has also used them as expert facilitators leading business and organizational strategic profiles for over two decades. Organizations such as the Y, Scouts, and 4H have used the approach for staff development, cultural orientation, and the learning and achievement of its members for generations. The military and law enforcement have used their experienced leaders to develop future leaders, in some cases, for centuries. Physicians are developed around the world using the adage, "see one, do one, teach one."

Figure 1.1 lists a sample of companies and organizations across many sectors that use the LAT approach.

Figure 1.1 - Sample of Companies and Organizations That Use the LAT Approach

Accenture	Dell	McCormick
Agilent Technologies	Deloitte	Merck
Alcoa	Defense Intelligence Agency (DIA)	Monsanto
Ameriprise Financial	GE	Novelis
Banner Health	General Mills	Procter & Gamble (P&G)
BD (Becton, Dickinson, and Company)	Hess	Raytheon
Boeing	Honeywell	Signature Healthcare
Caterpillar	HP (Hewlett Packard)	Southwest Airlines
Chevron	Kaiser-Permanente	UPS
Central Intelligence Agency (CIA)	3M	Wolterskluwer
Children's Healthcare of Atlanta	McCain-Foods	Y of Central Maryland

Evidence and Experience Suggests

There is an evolving body of evidence that suggests business, organizational, and individual value is realized when leaders serve as teachers. The following is a sample of current research on the topic. It is presented within the broader context of the importance that CEOs, boards of directors, and analysts currently place on human capital and strong company leadership.

Results From a 2013 Leaders as Teachers Study of the Conference Board Councils

In 2013, the authors administered a survey to three of the Conference Board councils. These councils are comprised primarily of the senior leaders of talent, learning, organization development, and leadership development of their respective companies and organizations. Participation was voluntary.

The following is a summary of the key findings from 22 participating companies.

- **Widespread Use:** About 90 percent of responders reported using a LAT approach for in-house leadership training programs. Additionally, nearly 30 percent use this approach for technical or business function training. About 15 percent are currently updating or expanding their LAT programs.

- **LAT Program Benefits:** When asked what benefits are derived from using a LAT approach they told us the following:
    - 70 percent volunteered that LAT contributed in a significant way to the development of employees and emerging leaders.
    - In 60 percent of the companies, LAT programs are viewed as helping to strengthen organizational culture and communications.
    - 50 percent said the program helped the leader-teachers themselves develop and improve.
    - 40 percent volunteered that the LAT approach is a key to driving business results and strategic alignment.
    - 40 percent commented that LAT is an aid to succession planning and career development programs.
- **Measuring Impact:** When asked about measures that demonstrate the impact of LAT programs, 65 percent reported using Level 1 evaluations to assure quality and drive improvements. Most reported very strong anecdotal evidence of the positive impact LAT has on learning and application.
    - 30 percent of respondents report having done studies or scorecard analyses that demonstrate the value of LAT over non-LAT training programs.

The results of this survey suggest that the LAT approach has gained significant ground as a beneficial method for training and developing employees and the next generation of leaders. LAT supports business results and strategic alignment and furthers a company's culture and communications (Betof and Owens 2013).

Results From a 2013 Research Report Published by The Conference Board

The detailed 2013 study *The DNA of Leaders: Leadership Development Secrets* examined 19 companies that have been recognized as exemplar and top award winning organizations for their practices in developing leaders. Amongst their many findings was the trend that chief executives are helping to redefine notions of leadership. There has been a distinct shift away from standardized (often external, business school-centered) programs toward customized (often in-house, company-specific) programs that feature action learning as an important component and are tightly focused on nonnegotiable company values. Most interviewees stressed the importance of having senior leaders heavily involved in the design and execution of their programs and, 16 of the 19 human capital survey respondents said their CEOs were highly involved in senior programs (Ray and Learmond, 2013).

Results From a 2010 Research Report Published by the Human Capital Institute (HCI) and Lee Hecht Harrison

In the report, *Leaders Developing Leaders: Capitalizing on the Demographic Gift to Revive Your Leadership Program,* a survey of 35 items was distributed to approximately 10,000 HCI members. Completed surveys were received from 412 different organizations. In addition, several in-depth interviews were conducted with leadership development thought leaders from top leadership companies. To supplement the primary methods described above, HCI researchers also reviewed relevant information from a variety of secondary sources, including whitepapers, articles, books, interviews, and case studies. Highlights of this research include:

- Over the past few decades when organizations have implemented Leaders Developing Leaders programs effective implementation has led to increased employee engagement, increased productivity, and a stronger network and supply of organizational leaders.

- Succession planning, employee satisfaction, and company profitability have correspondingly increased with the successful implementation of strong leadership development programs with Leaders Developing Leaders at their core.

- More than half of survey respondents agreed or strongly agreed that current leaders in their organization postponed their retirement plans as a result of the recession. With the delay of senior executive retirements comes a demographic gift. This allows organizations to have additional time with seasoned executives and recruit them to actively participate in Leaders Developing Leaders programs before their retirement plans resume.

- The top three benefits companies derive from Leaders Developing Leaders programs are that they instill leadership values and skills, strengthen organizational culture and communication, and help drive business results by ensuring strategic business alignment between senior and emerging leaders.

- Of the companies surveyed, 40 percent of organizations subscribe to the philosophy that "All leaders are expected to teach and coach emerging leaders."

- In addition to several selected competencies and capabilities, the two most important criteria that should be used for selection as leader-teachers, as chosen by respondents, are leaders must be role models (81 percent) and leaders must have proven performance in the organization (73 percent).

- When companies struggle to implement a Leaders Developing Leaders program, it is often because of issues such as availability of time, accountability related to teaching and coaching, lack of proper skills and knowledge to teach, and lack of appropriate infrastructure and consistent leadership development strategy (Human Capital Institute 2010).

In the overview of the leadership development techniques section of the 2011 report, LAT was used by 76 percent of the top global companies for leaders.

—Aon/Hewitt 2011

Results From a Doctoral Thesis Study

In a 2010 doctoral thesis at the University of Pennsylvania, Joseph Steier, CEO of Signature Healthcare, explored the concept that knowledge and application of theories, principles, and methods of adult learning to teaching may be a core management competency needed for companies to improve employee reaction to learning, knowledge transfer, and behavior, as well as engagement, retention, and profitability.

The literature review and conceptual framework for this dissertation centered on the growing research termed "leaders as teachers" and further defined teaching competencies for leaders through a set of adult learning theories, principles, and methods. The application of this idea was tested through the creation and deployment of Signature Healthcare's educational training program for managers, which included web-based modules and activities linked to principles and methods of adult learning, learning styles, facilitation versus traditional teaching, effective teaching methods, improved communication, establishment of learning cohorts, and application and demonstration of teaching skills. To assess its impact on improving workplace learning and performance within the subject organization, a randomized experiment was conducted in which individual and organizational performance was evaluated using Kirkpatrick's Levels of Evaluation as the theoretical framework. The researcher examined how the new teaching competency for managers impacted the reactions to learning (Level 1), knowledge transfer (Level 2), key individual behaviors (Level 3), and collective operational performance including employee engagement, retention, and overall company profitability (Level 4) when managers deployed this new teaching competency within the normal course of business in the workplace. This competency extended from the formal training situations to all activities of daily business. Having this teaching competency eliminated the dependency on the corporate learning and development department for training materials and directives, which reduced costs. Further, Steier found that the leader-teachers improved their performance over time. Training that incorporated the new competency improved participant reaction to training, increased knowledge transfer, changed employee behavior to reduce resident falls, and positively affected aspects of employee engagement. Employee retention improved, and when applied to the entire organization a cost savings of $1.9M was realized (Steier 2010).

Developing Leaders in High-Tech Firms: What's Different and What Works

A 2010 research article by Robert Fulmer and Byron Hanson summarized how to develop leaders in 23 high-tech firms. In part, it concluded:

- An overwhelming majority (89 percent) said that developing leaders is an area of increasing importance.
- More than half (58 percent) reported that their senior management believes that the development of leaders is a high or very high priority.
- While respondents were confident that their firms are headed in the right direction, few are satisfied with their current level of success and professionalism.

Amongst their suggestions, based on the success of other large high-tech firms, was to engage executives as teachers and facilitators who add value through their experience, observation, and feedback. Another recommendation was to leverage peer coaching, which is another form of leader as teacher, as a practical and receptive method to developing coaching capability (Fulmer and Hanson 2010).

Overview of the Action Guide

This action guide is the follow up to the book *Leaders as Teachers: Unlock the Teaching Potential of Your Company's Best and Brightest*, which was published in 2009. The book describes "what" to do, both on a broad scale and at a detailed level, through the use of case studies, checklists, and creative suggestions. It also provides a high-level "how" to do it that the Action Guide takes to the next level of specificity. The LAT Action Guide incorporates lessons we have learned, especially in the five years since LAT was published. Importantly, we have had access to more than 25 companies and organizations that currently have active leaders-as-teachers processes in place.

The overarching success formula is not complicated. Simply stated, winning companies simultaneously focus on strategies that grow their top line, bottom line, and talent pipeline.

The **leaders-as-teachers** approach has become an important factor supporting each of these three areas, which are vital for success in a very wide cross-section of today's businesses and organizations. What began as a custom of elders transmitting rituals, values, and stories centuries ago has evolved into powerful leadership, teaching, cultural, and communication assets for contemporary organizations.

 Your Turn

Jot down your thoughts on the following topics.

What aspects of the seven LAT principles are relevant to your situation?

_____

_____

_____

What will help engage others in the leaders-as-teachers approach from (a) a historical perspective, (b) evidence and experience, and (c) company and organizational examples?

_____

_____

_____

Choose Your Starting Plan

"Inch by inch, row by row, gonna make this garden grow. All it takes is a rake and a hoe and a piece of fertile ground…"

—*The Garden Song*, written by David Mallett

Find Your Answers

LAT initiatives can begin as one training program in one part of an organization, or can be launched across an entire enterprise. In this chapter you will read about elements that can drive each type of program and examples of program structures to support it. As you read, think about your answers to these questions:

- What is the scope for your LAT work?
- What business drivers and performance issues are present in your organization that can be addressed through a LAT initiative?
- Which of the LAT structures, described here, might be appropriate for your organization?
- How will you formulate a proposal for a new or expanded LAT approach in your workplace?

Starting plans for a LAT approach will vary based on a few factors: primarily who supports the approach and what business drivers are impacting the organization at the moment. A LAT approach might be proposed by a valued learning professional, or requested by a senior leader in the organization. The impetus for LAT might come as an outgrowth of a successful town hall meeting, in which employees engaged in a question and answer session with senior leaders, and expressed a desire for more of this type of interaction. The business drivers for a LAT approach might include a need for a new business strategy, alignment with the current strategy, strengthening the leadership pipeline, launching one or more new products, initiating significant change within the organization, improving organizational communications and culture, or a need to improve competency in one or more areas.

Use the Learn By Doing activity on the next page to determine your starting point rating. What does your rating mean? Whether your current rating is zero or 45, this book is here to help you grow or expand LAT. The Starting Point Assessment simply provides one important early indicator of the size and scope of LAT approach that your organization might be ready to accept at this time. If you have LAT in place, the assessment can suggest the organization's readiness to grow the LAT approach. And, if you and others are experiencing the benefits of LAT and want to expand the program to a new level, the Starting Point Assessment rating can provide insights into the need for additional processes and support structures to sustain success as you expand. Just keep in mind, the goal is to maximize LAT benefits, and characterize the current state—not to maximize an assessment score. Think of your goal as trying to get the biggest harvest out of your garden, no matter its size.

What LAT Size and Scope Is Right for My Situation?

Using the garden analogy, a small LAT plan is like planting a seed and nurturing it so that it matures, is enjoyed, adds value, and self-seeds more of the same in other locations. A medium LAT plan suggests planting a wider variety of seeds as the gardener learns more about what grows and what doesn't in this environment. A large LAT plan is characterized by a well-designed, more complex growing area that is highly supported by many of the resources, tools, and materials needed to cover a broad area of the organization.

Learn By Doing: Starting Point Assessment

Use the chart below to help you sort through the factors that may impact your organization's readiness levels for LAT. There are no right or wrong answers. Your responses simply reflect your understanding and assessment of the current state of readiness for LAT in your organization.

Indicator	Yes	Somewhat	No
Supportive People			
• Senior leaders across my organization requested a LAT approach.			
• Learning professionals in my organization want a LAT approach.			
• Leadership has provided sufficient funding for LAT programs.			
• Employees have expressed positive response to past LAT programs.			
Business Drivers			
• Alignment of business goals and strategy is needed.			
• Increasing or maintaining employee engagement and trust is critical at this time.			
• Significant organizational change is planned or occurring.			
• Skills and competencies need to be developed or increased.			
• Organizational culture must be strengthened—maybe across organizational silos.			
• Training cost-effectiveness is very important at this time.			
Tally the number of marks in each column.			
Multiply by the value here; enter the result on next line.	x 5	x 3	x 0
Rating (the sum of the first two columns):			

Use your Starting Point Assessment score and Figure 2.1 to help you determine what size and type of LAT plan is best suited for your organization at this time. As you look at your assessment, what do you think and how do you feel about the level of LAT readiness indicated for you and your organization. Do you agree? Disagree? During the process of validating this assessment across numerous companies and organizations, we've seen that most start with the "plant a seed" or "several rows" approach. If done well, growth to a few more "garden rows" is a common outcome as **leader-teachers** experience for themselves the multitude of benefits from the LAT approach. It is from this "inch by inch, row by row" starting position that most companies and organizations experience their initial LAT success and lay the foundation for larger growth and change.

Figure 2.1: Growing Your LAT Garden

Use the Starting Point Assessment score to suggest a starting plan for your LAT approach.

Plant a Seed	**Plant a Garden Row**	**Build a Garden Plan**
		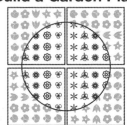
A Town Hall Meeting One Training Activity One Training Topic	Series on a Crucial Topic Set of Topics for One Goal	Most Topics, Most Places All Levels, Each Crucial Goal
Under 30, Plant a Seed	30-40, Plant a Garden Row	40-50, Build a Garden Plan

For ratings at the cusp (±1) consider a customized hybrid.

Continuing the analogy, no matter what size plan you start with, even the large garden plan begins with planting a single seed in a single row. The difference is the speed at which the garden can be completed, and the number of seasons over which the gardener can learn what works best in this environment. We highly recommend starting any LAT approach in a step-by-step manner. Grow the initiative only as fast as you can ensure success in each offering. Success begets success in an inch-by-inch, row-by-row manner. Even one highly visible program that is disappointing can negate a number of successful ones. We are not believers in a "big bang" change process when introducing a LAT approach. Nothing builds support and momentum better than successful programs where participants and the teaching faculty of leaders experience significant value from the learning experience.

Consider this: If you plant a LAT seed or a garden row today, by next year your LAT garden may have grown. If you already have LAT in place, reflect on how your Starting Point Assessment rating has changed since those initial days. You may be able to accelerate your LAT growth initiatives as a result.

Insights From Learning Professionals

"Whoever is going to champion the LAT program, they have to believe in it. There is a lot of work up front to convince people that this is the right way to go. In my experience, it's not going to feel natural to the leaders; it's not going to feel natural to the CEO. It can be pretty tricky to convince them. It could be viewed as the chiefs spending valuable time away from the office, and now they view it as an important part of the work because the 1,200 employees will benefit, so the whole company benefits. It's important to go slow, get a few victories, and then grow from there. That's the approach I took, and it worked. We started with two leader-teachers and grew to more than 20. Now, LAT is the way we do our important training at SES."

—Doug Clayton, Senior VP of HR, SES
For more on the SES story, see Chapter 12

Select a Support Structure

We all want our LAT learning programs to thrive and grow. Whether we plant a seed, a row, or a fuller garden plan, certain support structures can boost success and growth. When choosing an organizing structure, it helps to first decide what is needed. Figure 2.2 provides a list of things that are commonly required for varying sizes of LAT programs.

Figure 2.2: Common Components of Each Size of LAT Approach

Plant a Seed	Plant a Garden Row	Build a Garden Plan
• Use leader-teachers to supplement training facilitators. • Use subject matter experts (could be the leader-teachers). • Involve learning professionals to develop an active learning experience using active teaching methods. • Designate someone to manage logistics (invitations, room, or webinar scheduling, etc.). • Assign a coach to prepare leader-teachers for delivering the learning experience. • Employ a learning professional who will support the leader-teachers. • Designate a program owner or champion who will communicate the results of the learning events and encourage more of the same.	• Do everything in the Plant a Seed column. • Develop oversight to manage consistency and minimize redundancy. • Determine a method to get the right people to the right learning experiences. • Create a plan to assure a leader-teacher is available for each learning experience. • Develop a scorecard system to drive annual results analysis for the program. • Create an intentional plan to develop and grow each leader-teacher's teaching skills.	• Do everything in the Plant a Garden Row column. • Create a set of consistent practices to facilitate leader-teachers moving between programs. • Develop a structure to take advantage of economies of scale (LMS, printing standards, webinar software and support, contracts with external learning development suppliers, etc.). • Design a structured plan to build bench strength for future leader-teachers (a succession plan).

There are many ways to structure the support and governance for each program size. Here are a few examples to guide you as you develop your own LAT systems.

Plant a Seed Structure

While this structure is the simplest, it must be the strongest because it stands alone in the field. There must be at least one person who is a champion of both the topic and the LAT approach, as visualized in Figure 2.3. This person might be a senior leader or learning professional. Beyond that, there is a need for a person with a strong inclination for creating an **active teaching** design to deliver the content and message in a way that will cause participants to change their behavior in the workplace. Lastly, there is a need for someone who is excellent at managing all the detailed logistics needed for any major meeting or training. The Plant a Seed team might be just two people, but is more typically a learning professional with great administrative support and at least two or three leader-teachers.

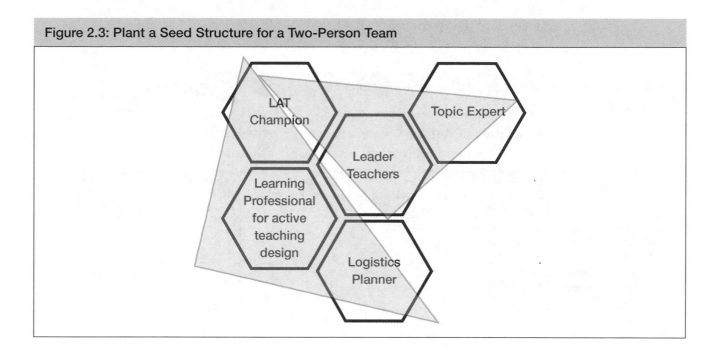

Figure 2.3: Plant a Seed Structure for a Two-Person Team

Plant a Garden Row Structure

This structure is characterized by a partnership between learning professionals and business leaders. Together, they set up a means of managing consistency, quality, and staffing for a topic or across a career level or business, as shown in Figure 2.4. The topic might be a core competency area, such as innovation or strategic thinking, or it might be a set of skills critical and unique to the business. Some learning programs that use the LAT approach will select a structure that manages only down the vertical, while others manage only on the horizontal. Those LAT-infused learning programs that are trending toward a Garden Plan may be managing both the horizontal and vertical.

The key for the Garden Row Structure is to form a partnership between learning professionals and leader-teachers to assure that the right people in the right departments are getting the right messages for their area of responsibility. Learning professionals can help leader-teachers by regularly providing a clear view of how deeply and broadly the content is being shared within the organization. The leader-teachers are responsible for being aware of organizational changes, business goals, and landscape trends that suggest a change in the breadth or depth of penetration or a change in the content. Together, learning professionals and leader-teachers assure that participants get just the right amount of learning that is pertinent to their success of the business.

Figure 2.4: Garden Row Structure With Rows or Columns

Sponser: Business Leader (C-level preferred)
Learning Program Champion: Senior Business Leader
Learning Profession: HR or Training Manager

	Owner of Competency or Key Skill A	Owner of Competency or Key Skill B	Owner of Competency or Key Skill C	Owner of Competency or Key Skill D	Owner of Competency or Key Skill E
Supporter or Stakeholder for Level 1 or Department 1	Content Owner/ Leader-Teachers				
Supporter or Stakeholder for Level 2 or Department 2		Content Owner/ Leader-Teachers			
Supporter or Stakeholder for Level 3 or Department 3			Content Owner/ Leader-Teachers		
Supporter or Stakeholder for Level 4 or Department 4				Content Owner/ Leader-Teachers	
Supporter or Stakeholder for Level 5 or Department 5					Content Owner/ Leader-Teachers

Build a Garden Plan Structure

The key differentiator of a Garden Plan is the addition of support structures for leader-teachers and the LAT-related learning events. The need for this addition becomes apparent when there are repeated requests for expensive infrastructure or proactive leader-teacher support and succession planning. By adding support structures, the organization can take advantage of economies of scale.

Common infrastructure items include a **learning management system** (LMS) or on enterprise-wide contract for a web-based training platform. Sometimes this common infrastructure is a physical building filled with training studios, classrooms, small-group study or breakout rooms, support staff offices, and possibly a dining area.

Many companies today have an LMS to track learners and the topics they need to learn or have already learned. These powerful computer applications can be harnessed to support LAT learning events. We encourage using an LMS to assure that leader-teachers and learning professionals have been identified for each upcoming event, along with the necessary resources, such as a webinar studio, passcode access for online programs, or reservations for a classroom. The LMS can also aid you in collecting data for a LAT learning program year-end report. This data might include the percentage of leaders at each level who have participated as a leader-teacher in one or more programs or events, as well as the number of employees and learners the leader-teachers have interacted with.

As the number of leader-teachers grows, it can be helpful to add several features to support them directly. A high-leverage item is the addition of leader-teacher staffing as an intentional part of executive talent development. This might be as simple as asking a leader to teach a different set of content to expand her knowledge base, or to teach the same content in a different part of the company to broaden her organizational knowledge and the scope of her influence. It might include adding a brief description of the leaders' recent leader-teacher contributions to promotion announcements.

Other leader-teacher support may include such things as classes to help develop teaching skills, a system for matching leader-teachers with skilled webinar co-pilots or producers, and contracts with proven external companies that can assist with learning event design, printing, material revisions, and graphic design. We also recommend an annual planning session to match leader-teachers to one or more learning events throughout the upcoming year.

Your LAT Proposal and Plans

LAT always includes planting seeds that eventually grow into rows, and might even expand into a large plot. We encourage you to move forward slowly and learn the lay of the land as you go. The goal is not to get the biggest garden, but to get the biggest fruit from each plant, that is to say, the most benefit and value from each learning event involving leader-teachers.

There are many ways to get started. You might begin by having conversations with leader-teachers to plant the seed during informal discussions or meetings. You could also write your thoughts and ideas in a formal proposal, using the template for an LAT Proposal provided at the end of this chapter. Regardless of how you get started, begin growing your garden now so you can begin to reap the benefits of your LAT approach.

 **Your Turn**

Jot down your thoughts on the following topics.

What is the scope for the organization's LAT approach today? Is the scope likely to change in the next few years?

_____

_____

What business drivers and performance issues are pressing right now, that a LAT approach could help to address?

_____

_____

What structure might best support your LAT program now and in the coming years? What elements of this structure are already in place? What elements need to be created?

_____

_____

What proposals need to be developed and accepted to gain alignment on a new or expanded LAT approach? Who will develop these? By when? What elements of the LAT Proposal Template (below) might you use?

_____

_____

LAT Proposal Template

This template can get you started on developing your own recommendation to implement or expand a LAT approach where you work. The brackets [ ] suggest what type of content to type as you customize the recommendation. A slash indicates a choice of words. Choose what works best in your situation.

Naturally, if your organization has a standard recommendation format for business proposals, your company's own business template should be used, and the LAT template might help as you formulate your recommendations and proposed plan. This template assumes that the recommendation is unsolicited, and can be adjusted if this recommendation is in response to a request from someone within the organization, such as a senior leader or a senior learning professional or talent development leader.

To: [Sponsor or approving body]

From: [Your Name or Team Name, i.e., The Leaders as Teachers Study Team]

Subject: Addressing [business issue or business goal] Through a Leaders-as-Teachers Approach

This recommends that [we/organization name/company name] implement a leaders-as-teachers approach as one component to help address [business issue/goal/need].

Business Issue/Need: The business is facing/striving for [specify the business issue/goal need]. [Indicate your familiarity with the business issue by commenting on what has already been done or planned to address the issue.] [Identify the gaps remaining in the solution, or the elements that can be enhanced by applying a LAT approach.]

- **Description of a Leaders-as-Teachers Approach/Solution:** [Describe the LAT program that would address the issue/goal. It might be setting up learning events that are delivered by leader-teachers across a specific time/region, adding leader-teacher involvement in an existing program, or one of many ideas described in this book.]

Benefits: [Select 1-3 benefits of the LAT approach for this business issue that will be most important to the reader. We recognize that you will likely envision additional benefits, but select those few benefits that are most closely aligned with your company's or organization's concerns or goals. See the six most common benefits below.]

- **Help drive business results.** When senior leaders design and deliver learning events, it can drive business results by aligning the learning programs with the most pertinent strategies, goals, and outcomes.
- **Stimulate learning and development:** Leader-teachers build everyone's capabilities, serve as role models, and reinforce the organization's core values. Participants have opportunities to practice skills and behaviors in a safe classroom environment and to receive feedback from leaders with whom they would not normally interact. This encourages creative problem-solving and allows participants to build relationships that can be important resources for their personal career development.
- **Improve leadership skills for leader-teachers.** Leader-teachers report that they gain more knowledge of the content they teach; hone their own unique leadership perspective (ULP) on the issues most important to them, which better prepares them to model desired leadership behavior in their fulltime roles; and benefit from considering the different perspectives of participants, especially in diverse groups representing different parts of the organization.

- **Strengthen organizational culture and communications.** The LAT approach bolsters organizational lines of communication by providing tools to raise issues and solve problems. When the learning events involve diverse groups of participants, LAT fosters cross-functional and cross-cultural ties.
- **Promote positive business and organizational change.** Leader-teachers help prepare participants for change, and can benefit by becoming intimately aware of concerns that have not yet been brought to light. As these concerns surface, leader-teachers can guide teams to make needed modifications or reduce barriers, thereby increasing the likelihood of the change program succeeding.
- **Reduce costs of L&D programs.** Leader-teachers can serve as subject-matter experts in lieu of expensive external consultants.

Next Steps: [specify timing and who will take the initiative to complete each of the items below]

- **Gain agreement:** [Indicate how you and the sponsor will come to agreement — will an email approving the work be sufficient? Are you planning to meet? Do you need the sponsor to review this recommendation with others?]
- **Information gathering:** [List the information that needs to be collected to further frame the LAT approach. For example, get a count of the number of participants involved, conduct interviews with senior leaders to determine who has inherent interest in being a leader-teacher, or estimate the costs and savings associated with LAT.]
- **Resources:** [Indicate what resources you will need to carry out the suggested plan for LAT. This might be a budget issue, or a request for a leader-teacher to begin working with you. Consider attaching a rough schedule if it would be helpful to drive a sense of urgency.]

[May we have your agreement to proceed? Or can we discuss this further (meeting time)?]

[Individual or group name]

Form Your LAT Team

"Begin with the end in mind."

—Stephen Covey

■ ■ ■

 ## Find Your Answers

This chapter provides a guide for bringing together and leading a team of people who will grow your organization's LAT culture. As you read, think about your answers to these questions.

- What is the purpose of your LAT team? And, given that purpose, who should be on your team? What roles could they take on?
- How can you leverage the power of "going to the light" to help you recruit members for your LAT team and faculty? How can you help others view LAT work as a valid part of their job, rather than an extra obligation?
- Once you have formed a LAT team, what's next?

In the last chapter you determined the extent of your leaders-as-teachers program. The next step is to engage others to bring your LAT vision to life. It helps to list the various roles that are needed, and then list people who might be able and willing to fill one or more roles. In this chapter we will explore some approaches that others have used to successfully identify people for their LAT team, recruit them, and help the **leader-teachers** grow within their roles. These approaches will also help you develop the leader-teacher pipeline, as well as personally aid leader-teachers as they grow their skill set, and as they take on more complex or specialized leader-teacher roles.

Your LAT Team

First and foremost, *you* are part of the LAT team. Consider what role you will take, which roles you will delegate, or which you will need to fill by other means. In order to be realistic about the size of the role you can perform well, consider the size of the program—seed, row, or garden. Taking the analogy a step further, are you the landowner or the gardener? Perhaps you are the horticultural expert or the person who hires those who will harvest the field. None of these roles are insignificant. Each one takes time and energy, and is an important element in producing a great outcome—a harvest of participants who are well prepared to achieve the strategic goals that have been set out for the organization. The role of learning professionals is crucial to the success of any LAT approach. Take that as a given and enroll those experts. With that assumption in place, we will focus on identifying, recruiting, and growing the leader-teacher members of the LAT team.

Tailor the list in the Learn By Doing activity on the next page to your situation. Figure 3.1 lists a few additional roles to consider. We leave it to you to craft names for these roles as befits your organizational culture.

Figure 3.1: Examples of Additional Leader-Teacher Roles	
• Be a program champion, with overall program responsibilities such as staffing, budget, and continuous improvement. Help conduct and analyze an organizational performance study.	• Provide video recorded messages for various programs. Lead or co-lead the development of a new program, perhaps as a subject matter expert.
• Be a topic champion, with responsibilities for a topic or competency to assure that a consistent message is delivered across each appropriate level and organization.	• Be an advisor to help customize programs for a region or department.
• Serve as a corporate university dean of a "college" that clusters a family of topics into one larger program.	• Advise on the selection of external or off-the-shelf training programs, and possibly teach one of these after completing an in-house program.
• Serve as the corporate university president or leader on a global or regional level.	• Be an active blogger for a program, or regularly review online comments and post additional perspectives.
	• Conduct webinars.

Learn By Doing:
Match Roles to Leader-Teachers

Use the columns below to list the roles that will support your LAT approach. We've listed some basic roles to get you started. See Chapter 2 for other roles and titles that are relevant to the purpose of your LAT initiative. Next, fill in some names of people who might fill whose roles. Pencil in some lines connecting people to the roles they might fill.

Matching Roles to People Template	
Roles to Fill	**Potential People**
• LAT Sponsor: Leader-Teacher (supports and leads the LAT approach)	
• LAT Sponsor: Learning Professional (supports and leads the LAT approach)	
• Learning Professional for Active Design	
• Logistics Planner(s)	
• Topic Expert(s)/SMEs (list by topic)	
• Leader-Teachers (list by topic)	
• Program or College Leader/Facilitator	
• Technology Coordinator/Master	
• Others:	

Figure 3.2 is an example of a completed Matching Roles to People template. Use your initial draft of the template to help you identify gaps in the People column. In the early stages of forming a LAT approach or culture, a general call for volunteers is typically not helpful. Rather, consider filling the gaps using one of these three approaches, each of which falls under the umbrella principle of **go to the light:** desired-performance dialogs, probing interviews on business challenges, and nomination by expertise. No matter what approach you use, be sure to focus on a business need and, thereby, set the tone for the LAT approach—that LAT is a method for driving business results!

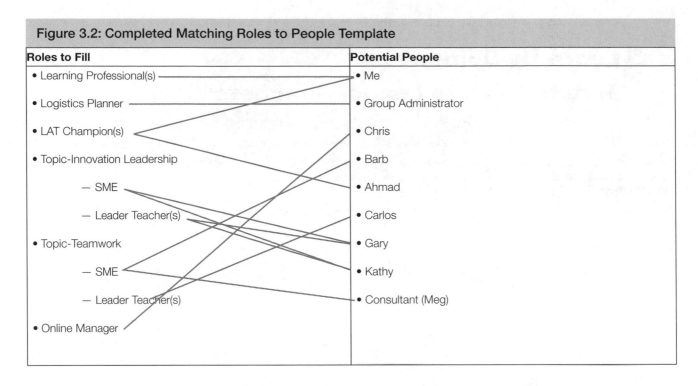

Figure 3.2: Completed Matching Roles to People Template

Roles to Fill	Potential People
• Learning Professional(s)	• Me
• Logistics Planner	• Group Administrator
• LAT Champion(s)	• Chris
• Topic-Innovation Leadership	• Barb
— SME	• Ahmad
— Leader Teacher(s)	• Carlos
• Topic-Teamwork	• Gary
— SME	• Kathy
— Leader Teacher(s)	• Consultant (Meg)
• Online Manager	

The Go to the Light Principle

This principle is simple but very powerful. To successfully initiate a new organization process such as leaders as teachers, tap into sources of personal and organizational energy in the form of interests, growth opportunities, problems, and concerns. Specifically, identify people who have strong personal interests in teaching, coaching, and facilitation, and seek out strong business growth opportunities or problems that need to be solved for which teaching and learning is part of the solution.

To use the go to the light principle, talk with leaders about the LAT approach. Watch for clear signs of interest, such as shining eyes and excited dialog. Know your organization. Where are the business opportunities? What are the problems, concerns, and obstacles that the organization is facing? All of these are reservoirs of untapped organizational energy that provide access to initiating or expanding a LAT approach to address these interests, opportunities, and problems. This personal approach can be very effective. Talk to leaders about your leader-teacher ideas every chance you get, whether it is in the boardroom, on airplanes, at the fitness center, or in cafeteria lines. Plant seeds of ideas wherever you are. Enroll those leaders who demonstrate a spark of energy or passion for this approach.

Desired-Performance Dialogs

These conversations tend to be more formal discussions about raising performance to achieve a business goal. For example, the business need might be to increase strategic thinking among mid-level managers, or to get new hires on-boarded more quickly. As each meeting progresses, look for leaders who may have a hidden talent for creating action learning and simulation learning activities. Look for leaders who want to roll up their sleeves and get involved to make a change.

Probing Interviews

This approach involves a series of leader interviews on such topics as preparing for the future or meeting a new competitive marketplace challenge. As they uncover the elements of the business challenge, watch for those leaders who appear to have the energy to resolve those challenges.

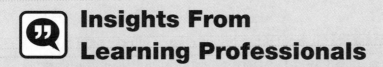

Insights From Learning Professionals

"We have involved our leadership in developing training right from the start. In fact, one of our senior vice presidents requested that we develop a training program. Our leadership was very willing to help us identify training needs and priorities. We never considered asking them to teach. However, during a series of interviews, our interviewer asked the question, 'Would you be interested in being a leader-teacher? Maybe in a classroom or perhaps as an online leader-teacher?' We were surprised by the positive responses. Several of our leaders were already teaching at local universities or had been leader-teachers at previous firms."

—Arlette Watwood, Cenovus Energy

Nomination by Expertise

This method of identifying leader-teachers involves canvassing senior leaders and peers of potential leader-teachers. Ask them, either at a group meeting or individually, which leaders they think are skilled at the topics that will be addressed in your LAT learning events or program. Probe the recommendations a bit. "Why do you think Joe is the right person to talk on this topic?" "What makes Mary stand out in your opinion?" "Do you think others will see Melissa as the expert?" Remember these narratives so that you can use them when you recruit the individuals. Of course, be aware of the confidential nature of your conversations, and share only what is appropriate. You are likely to find that, on a given topic, the same names will be mentioned again and again. These will be good people to recruit.

Now that you have a list of people who either exhibit a passion to be part of the LAT approach, or come recommended as unacknowledged experts on the topic, you are ready to move to the next step—recruiting.

How to Recruit Team Members

Two overarching principles will help you organize your leader-teacher recruiting efforts:

- Attract leader-teachers by matching potential teaching assignments with the leaders' background, expertise, responsibilities, and interests.
- Prepare leader-teachers to teach. Leaders will want to teach and will teach best when they are well prepared to teach effectively.

Once you have identified what roles need to be filled and the likely candidates for your LAT team, the next step is to make the offers. When you ask a leader to be involved in the LAT learning event or program, be prepared to answer these common questions:

- How much of my time will it take? Over what period of time?
- What is the scope of the role?
- Why me?
- Has my boss agreed to this?

Time

When asked about the time it will take, be prepared to answer the underlying questions: what day and hours do I need to block out on the calendar, what amount of thinking and preparation time is required, and is this is a one-time event or a long-term expectation?

If the learning event date conflicts with the leader-teacher's calendar, this is likely to be a very short discussion. Alternately, assure them that you will work with their calendar or set up pairs of trainers for each module for mutual support and for coverage in case of emergency business situations.

The amount of "think time" and preparation can be a major factor. For example, will the L&D staff provide support, or will the leader-teacher have to create materials on their own. While different organizations take different approaches, our experience is that leader-teachers appreciate working in partnership with L&D people to hone their messages and materials. If materials are already prepared, leader-teachers are often grateful when an L&D professional walks them through the materials to help them prepare more quickly. It is wise to involve L&D professionals in preparing the message and materials to assure that **active teaching** and active learning methods are used, as described in chapter 4.

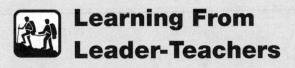

Learning From Leader-Teachers

When asked how he addressed the commonly heard complaint from leaders about being too busy to teach, John Leikhim, retired manager/VP of research and development at P&G, said: "It is the responsibility of leaders to develop their people. Do you or do you not agree, that it is part of your job to develop the people in your organizations? If you agree, there is no discussion. Now we can talk about scheduling, planning, and priorities." He went on to say that it really isn't that hard to teach. "This is about sharing your story—about the lessons learned and the principles you distilled from it. This is not Broadway. It's not as high a hurdle as people make it out to be. It really is about their ability to distill their experiences into principles and transfer that to their organizations, and that is a critical part of their job."

Some leader-teachers like roles that they can hold and develop over a period of several years. Others prefer a get-in-and-get-out approach, although they might be willing to teach the same materials and concepts annually for several years. This is the time to build relationships with your leader-teachers. Learn what they prefer and make a note of it. Help match roles to preferences as much as possible.

Scope

The question of scope is integrally intertwined with the "how much time" question. Be clear about what the role entails and what the responsibilities are. No one wants to commit to something only to discover that the commitment is much bigger than they were led to believe. Do not overstate or understate the work involved. Do focus on the support provided as well as the goals of the program and the benefits that can be achieved. If the goals and benefits are right, leaders make time to contribute as teachers.

Why Me?

The "why me?" question is important. Think about how the leader's name got on your list and share the narrative. Typically, the reason is one of two things. One, he is needed—as the leader, he is most equipped to deliver these messages. Two, she is considered by others to be an expert or skilled in an area or topic, although no one ever mentioned this to her. You have the opportunity to provide this positive feedback. We have experienced this phenomenon repeatedly, and interviews across companies have reinforced that this occurs frequently in many organizations. When someone is good at something, a leader-teacher culture provides an alternate avenue of providing positive and reinforcing feedback.

Manager's Agreement

The question, "Has my boss agreed to this?" can have several answers. This could be a chicken-and-egg issue, that is, do we gauge the individual's interest level first and then get their boss's agreement? Or is it the other way around? If there is no option except for this person to be part of the program, you can get the boss's agreement first. Understand, however, that this approach might squelch some natural enthusiasm for the role. The more energizing route is to tell the individual who the sponsor is for this program, and offer a note or conversation from the sponsor to the individual's boss to formally request his or her time and effort for this work. Most managers will agree, and many will actually be eager to make the LAT role a legitimate part of the work if teaching and facilitating is a personal area of interest or area of expertise. Their involvement also becomes much more natural to the extent that it is connected to driving business growth or addressing important organizational issues.

Expansion and Progression

Once your LAT program is established, typically over the course of several years, consider the need of leader-teachers to continue to grow or step up to new challenges. We recommend using a **progression** plan to encourage and aid key leaders to grow into new leader-teacher roles. Figure 3.3 provides ideas on different ways to look at the various types of progression you might pursue in your LAT program.

Figure 3.3: Types of Progression

Here are some paths for progress that we have encountered. As you look at the list of possible LAT roles in Figures 3.1 and 3.2, you may see additional possibilities for progression that would apply to your organization.

Part to Whole
- Co-trainer of a small part to solo trainer of more or all content to lead trainer coaching the next new leader-teacher
- Leader-teacher for a topic within a corporate university college to topic champion, or owner responsible for a small training team on one topic to college dean responsible for working with all topic champions to deliver the college programs

Reapplication in Different Area
- Leader-teacher for a topic to leader-teacher for a different topic
- Leader-teacher for a group of learners to leader-teacher for a different region or organization

Innovation
- Leader-teacher with existing program to leader-teacher who develops and hones new active learning methods
- Leader-teacher for classroom to leader-teacher who leads the way for conversion of face-to-face (f2f) to virtual learning events to leader-teachers who experiments with town halls for learning to leader-teacher who innovates the guided learning journey (GLJ, chapter 6) approach for your organization

Progress might take the form of being a leader-teacher for a larger portion of a learning program and doing it with increasingly less support from a co-trainer. Another progression is akin to moving to higher levels in an organization by taking on the responsibility to coordinate more topics, programs, and leader-teacher teams. Sometimes, simply moving to new topics or content is a broadening experience. Likewise, working with significantly different participant groups can be a new challenge. For example, teaching on the topic of innovation or strategy in the research and development department requires a different level of knowledge than teaching the same topic for the HR or manufacturing groups.

We encourage you to develop a progression for each leader-teacher, in much the same way as one might map out a career plan. The choices will depend on the individual's nature, their comfort level, and experience as a leader-teacher, their personal interests, and, as always, the driving business needs of the moment.

Learn By Doing:
Map Progression to Leader-Teachers

Once you have some LAT programs in place, list the names of people in current roles and jot down one or more roles that might engage and develop the individual. Note the type of progression—part to whole, re-application, or innovation.

Matching Roles to People Progression Template			
Roles to Fill	People in the Role	Next Role in the Progression	Type of Progression
• LAT Sponsor: Leader-Teacher • LAT Sponsor: Learning Professional • Learning Professional for Active Design • Logistics Planner(s) • Topic Expert(s)/ SMEs (topic) • Leader-Teachers (topic) • Program Leader/Facilitator • Technology Coordinator • Others:			

Quick Tip

In all that you do as part of the LAT approach, tap into the organization's core competencies and standard methods of operating: if your company is a marketing firm, be sure to market your LAT products internally; if it's a consumer-centric company, then treat your leader-teachers and participants as consumers; or, if you work for a company known for high service levels, duplicate that experience in the leader-teacher supported event.

Now That You Have an LAT Team, What's Next?

Having a LAT team is more than just having a set of leaders who do some training. Your LAT team is a valuable resource for insights into the business and the employees they will train. What does your organization teach about effective teams? Use that model for LAT teams. If there is no internal standard, consider using the model described in Figure 3.4.

Figure 3.4: Characteristics of Effective Teams

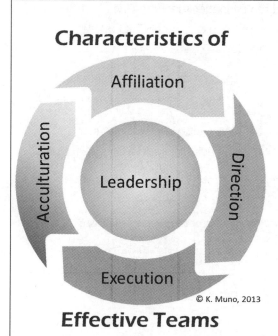

Affiliation—Team members know why they are part of the team, their unique roles and contributions, and how they are expected to engage and interact with others.

Direction—Each member understands and is guided by the vision, mission, goals, tasks, success criteria, timing, and resources necessary to deliver the team's results.

Execution—The team is guided by the processes needed to accomplish the tasks, such as planning, decision-making, tracking and control, and methods of meeting and communicating.

Acculturation—Team members acknowledge a culture supporting trust, celebrating success, and maintaining a focus on continual improvement and increased effectiveness over time.

Leadership—A single leader or shared leadership ensures the team is aligned to the direction, encourages inclusion, coaches to build capability, and inspires high performance to deliver results.

Depending on the nature of the team goals and the scope of the LAT work, LAT learning professionals might find themselves working with one very large team, or several smaller teams. Take the time to develop the characteristics of an effective team. Good teamwork does not happen overnight, or by decree. Developing an effective team is a process. Be ready to go through the stages to build a solid foundation to attain higher levels of performance.

Congratulations! You have completed your study and initial thought-development on step one, Framing Your Leaders as Teachers Approach and are starting step two, Making Your LAT Initiative Come Alive.

 ## Your Turn

Jot down your thoughts on the following topics.

What do you see as the primary purpose of your LAT team? Are you thinking more along the lines of a single team to develop and deliver a program against one business objective, or a larger team to cover multiple programs, or several teams to cover various programs?

_____

_____

What approaches might work best for you to select and recruit leader-teachers? Who can provide insights and recommendations as you gather a list of people to recruit? (Consider using the Matching Roles to People template.)

_____

_____

What are your thoughts about the effectiveness of your LAT team(s)? What elements of team effectiveness are in your control? Which elements might you ask others to manage?

_____

_____

Making Your LAT Initiative Come Alive

Part II is about building momentum for a **leaders-as-teachers** approach by using active learning methods, practicing teach in the moment skills, using social and collaborative learning technologies, creating a strong LAT brand, and applying a change management approach.

Chapter 4: Design Your Active Teaching Program

Learn about methods to help **leader-teachers** break out of the habit of using PowerPoint as a script, so that they can better engage learners. These methods include: learning frames, **unique leadership perspectives** (ULP), and visuals.

Chapter 5: Teach in the Moment

Encourage leaders to teach in the moment everyday as a powerful way to develop the next generation of leaders.

Chapter 6: Harness the Power of Collaborative Learning

Enroll and empower leader-teachers in online and virtual learning and collaboration.

Chapter 7: Establish Your Brand to Drive Business Results and Learning

Develop and deliver brand equity for your LAT initiative that can capture the hearts and minds of your company's best and brightest.

Chapter 8: Plan for Change and Build Momentum

Embed LAT in your culture using Kotter's classic eight-stage change management approach.

Chapter 4

Design Your Active Teaching Program

"When I hear it, I forget.
When I hear and see it, I remember…a little.
When I hear, see, ask questions about it, or discuss it
with someone else, I begin to understand.
When I hear, see, discuss, and do it, I acquire knowledge and skill.
When I teach it to another, I master."

—Mel Silberman, author, *Active Learning*

■ ■ ■

 Find Your Answers

In this chapter you will discover ways to introduce teaching methods that are more effective than the standard lecture mode. As you read, think about your answers to these questions:

- Which active teaching frames will be most likely to help leader-teachers effectively engage participants?
- What combination of active learning methods will provide variety and suit your culture?
- What support will leader-teachers need to help them develop their own unique leadership perspective (ULP), and use visuals for enhanced recall?

Each of us has our own experiences of content-heavy lectures and "death by PowerPoint." We've seen participants struggle to stay awake in such classes, trying not to embarrass themselves and their teachers. For many **leader-teachers,** the old lecture mode is the primary method they have experienced and therefore, the one they tend to model their own teaching approach on. How can we help leader-teachers teach differently? This chapter provides methods that have proven effective with leader-teachers: **active teaching** frames filled with active learning methods, ULP, and visuals for enhanced recall.

 Learning From Leader-Teachers

"When I was a new brand manager at P&G, it was assumed that people knew how to coach each other, but I wasn't sure I knew how. My HR manager, Carol Tuthill, helped me see that coaching and teaching are learned skills. She taught me a simple, concrete approach to learning or teaching something new: step one, observe a master; step two, have a master observe and give tips; and step three, do it on your own and report back to the master on the experience. There were lots of influences on what I wanted to be as a leader-teacher: Stephen Covey's concept of third-person teaching, Noel Tichy's idea of forming a "teachable point of view," P&G HR leader Gibby Carey's behavioral definition of leadership (the 5 Es), and former P&G CEO Bob McDonald's encouragement to develop a personal leadership philosophy. I applied this knowledge when I was appointed head of P&G's external relations department. One of my first initiatives was to engage our leaders in creating a new hire development program. It became a practical necessity for me and my leadership team to build our skills to teach, to create our own teachable point of view, and to deliver engaging case studies as well as our then CEO Ed Artzt, who was a master at it. We needed to make our knowledge available to others, especially to P&G people outside the Cincinnati area. And we had to do more than just tell our story—we had to inspire people to excel. Ultimately, a leader's skill as a teacher and coach became a point of differentiation for our very best leaders. It mattered."

—Charlotte Otto, Senior Corporate Strategist at Weber Shandwick and retired Global External Relations Officer, P&G (P&G 1976-2010)

Active Teaching Frames

An active teaching frame is a structure that can be used for a wide variety of content and situations (Thiagi 1994). Three frames, shown in Figure 4.1, have proven particularly successful with leader-teachers. A frame is constructed of blocks that can be filled with a wide variety of learning methods, such as small group activities, flip chart assignments, and case study exercises.

As you work with each leader-teacher or design each learning block, a good way to begin is to select an active teaching frame that is suited to the content, then fill it with learning methods that are a good match to the leader-teachers' style. Figure 4.2 provides a template that we have found useful for this design work, followed by an example. Additional examples are available at the end of the chapter.

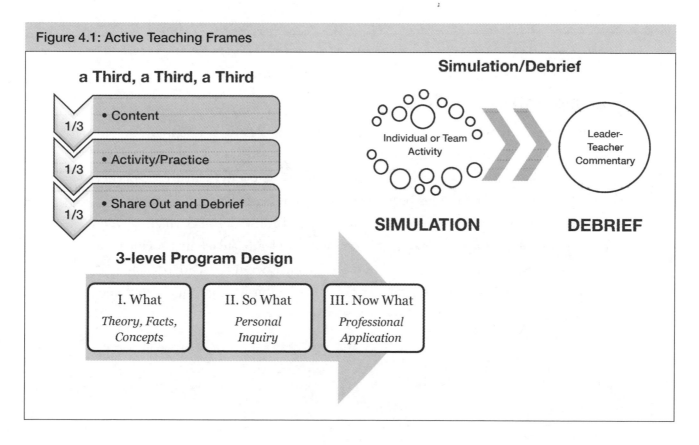

Figure 4.1: Active Teaching Frames

a Third, a Third, a Third

- 1/3 • Content
- 1/3 • Activity/Practice
- 1/3 • Share Out and Debrief

Simulation/Debrief

Individual or Team Activity

Leader-Teacher Commentary

SIMULATION   **DEBRIEF**

3-level Program Design

I. What	II. So What	III. Now What
Theory, Facts, Concepts	*Personal Inquiry*	*Professional Application*

Figure 4.2: Active Teaching Design Template	
Title of Learning Program or Segment:_____	
Active Teaching Frame: _____	
Active Learning Methods:	
a.	d.
b.	e.
c.	f.
Description:	

A Third, a Third, a Third

In this frame, the first third is when leader-teachers deliver essential content. Encourage leader-teachers to use an active learning method to deliver this content or to keep it under 10 minutes. The second third is an activity in which participants apply the content. This part typically takes at least as long as the first part, if not longer. The final, and most important third is the debrief, which is when participants share the outcome of their activity and leader-teachers provide positive and constructive feedback and reinforcement. Encourage leader-teachers to reserve plenty of class time for the debrief, because this is when their experience and wisdom can be best showcased.

Example of a Completed Active Teaching Design Template

Title of Training: Thinking Strategically to Innovate

Frame: A Third, a Third, a Third

Active Learning Methods:

a. Storytelling

b. Problem Solving

c. Peer Teaching

Description:

During the first third, a leader-teacher briefly introduces the newly developed in-house proprietary model that encourages strategic thinking to drive innovation. Then a world-renown external expert in innovation tells several stories about failures to innovate that would have been prevented with the use of this model. The leader-teacher facilitates a collaborative experience to help participants make parallels to the company projects, language, structures, and situations. The participants are deeply engaged in their learning.

During the second third, participants apply the new model working in small teams, where each team is assigned a different innovation challenge in different parts of the business. The teams develop a set of action steps that can drive innovation in those businesses. During this period, the pair of leader-teachers rotates among the teams to answer questions or intervene and redirect if the team seems to be heading down a blind alley. They may also pose questions such as "what if…" or "had you considered…" to drive a more sophisticated or informed solution.

During the final third, the teams present their approach to the other participants, answer questions, and share their rational. Each team has a unique way of applying the same model. The pair of leader-teachers adds their commentary. Sometimes, a leader-teacher will even reveal some of what they heard going on within the small team setting. (Naturally, these revelations are done with care, to avoid embarrassment for individuals or teams.) Leader-teachers might describe the struggles they observed within some of the teams to help the larger class understand that such struggles and difficult conversations are normal and beneficial to a good outcome.

See the end of the chapter for examples of the other two frames.

Simulation/Debrief

This frame is designed by starting with the end in mind. Design an activity that simulates the workplace in a way that causes participants to apply the necessary skill or competency to successfully complete the simulation. After participants complete the simulation, the leader-teacher leads the debrief, asking questions such as, "What was supposed to happen? What actually happened? What would you do differently if you did this again?" During a good debrief, experienced leader-teachers tend to do more listening than talking, using questions, comments, and real-life stories to make critical connections between the activity and the workplace.

The Three-Level Program Design

This frame divides the learning into three progressive elements that answer the questions "what," "so what" and "now what." It emphasizes the transfer of learning from theory to insight and then to practice and implementation. In the "what" segment, provide facts, concepts, or theories to be learned. Leader-teachers might do this via video, interview, or written document as alternatives to a lecture. Participants might take in this material individually or as a small-group activity. In the "so what" segment, participants work through the meaning of the facts/content/theory as it applies to them. Again, use any active learning method to help participants think through the answers to questions such as, "What is the importance of this to me?" "What is the value of this for me and my team?" In the "now what" segment, participants determine if and how they will apply the content in the workplace, mapping out answers to such questions as, "How can I apply what I have learned?" "What do I want to implement and why?" and "What is my implementation plan and my initial steps?" This frame drives dry theory to engaged action in the workplace.

 Quick Tip

Guide leader-teachers toward higher levels of active learning with this "rule of thumb" that they can apply to their training: Aim for at least 50 percent active learning with participants doing something beyond simple listening. A stretch goal is 80 percent active learning.

Insights From Learning Professionals

"I had one leader who just wasn't comfortable with the normal teaching mode. But all our leaders needed to be teachers at that time. With a bit of frustration, I asked, 'So what's on your desk? What are you working on?' He picked up a thick folder and said, 'I'm working on a possible acquisition.' His eyes lit up. 'I could give this to the participants and they could go through the process and decide if we should buy this company,' he said. It worked. He wasn't the kind of leader who would be a great orator, but he could very effectively talk about his work. Thankfully, the content he had to offer matched the mission for one of our learning events, so it worked well for all of us."

—Kevin D. Wilde, VP, Organizational Effectiveness & CLO, General Mills, speaking of his early career experience as a learning professional at GE's Crotonville.

Active Learning Methods

For each part of the active teaching frame, guide leader-teachers to select active learning methods that match their personal style. While the options are essentially limitless, a few examples are listed in the next Learn By Doing activity.

Because there is a tendency for people to believe that if they are teaching they must be talking, be sure to point out to the leader-teacher what they should be doing during activities. At a minimum, coach leader-teachers to listen in during activities and start selecting stories that will appeal to the group while enhancing their learning, and to start mapping out key points to cover in the debrief.

Learn By Doing: Active Learning

As you read this list, jot down the names of leader-teachers who might enjoy and effectively use the method.

Active Learning Method	Good for a Leader-Teacher who:	Leader-Teacher
Interactive Lectures: The leader-teacher lectures while the participants do a task. For example, individually, as learning partners, or in small groups, take periodic "time outs" to develop headlines or major learning points. Or have participants use "mind mapping" software on their computer or create mind maps by hand to capture the key points of the lecture. Every 10 minutes, stop and ask participants to summarize the key points by explaining a part of the mind map to a teammate or get a few volunteers to share with the class.	• is a subject matter expert and can talk at length on the topic • prefers to be in control of the room rather than manage the back-and-forth dialog across an entire class • might need a learning professional to watch the class and observe when a break in the lecture would be a benefit • has a lot of content that the participants must process in a very short time frame	
Small Group Work: The class is divided into small groups to work on a task, such as having a discussion, responding to case studies, solving a problem, or some other predesigned exercise or simulation.	• can interactively engage in dialog in small group settings • could benefit from learning more about a topic by hearing multiple groups' perspectives	
Social Media and Technology: In this emerging learning space, leader-teachers periodically go online to review and add to topical dialog. The leader-teacher commentary reinforces good thinking, acknowledges participants, adds perspective to some discussions, and collaborates on emerging solutions.	• has little time to participate in scheduled classes • can benefit from social collaborative problem solving on a business issue	
Town Hall Meetings: A leader meets with a group from about twenty to several hundred or more people. The town hall meeting usually begins with the leader providing a business, functional, or project update. This is frequently done in 10-15 minutes. The remaining time is spent responding to questions posed by participants in-person or virtually if social media and virtual communications are employed. This latter technique is sometimes referred to as a group interview. This method can also be used as a separate active learning method.	• can address a large group while demonstrating confidence and presence • is willing to respond in the moment and perhaps show personal authenticity as well as vulnerability	
Visual Metaphorical Facilitation: In this approach, the leader uses photographs, digital images, film clips, and other visual forms as metaphors to tell and have participants tell stories, share unique leadership perspectives, and to facilitate both logical and creative and divergent thinking.	• appreciates symbolic thinking • could benefit from a less factual approach • encourages lateral, divergent, and creative thinking and self-expression	
Webinar. A leader-teacher provides the primary content using short-bursts of lecture while trained web-facilitators manage the technology and the participants' engagement through online chats, surveys, and quizzes.	• has a dispersed workforce or travels frequently • is an effective lecturer on a topic	

Learning From Leader-Teachers

"When I first started teaching, I thought it was like doing a speech. My job was to arrive on time, give my talk, answer a few questions, and leave. Teaching, I've come to realize, is quite different. I still have to arrive on time, but the similarities end there. When I give my talk, I have to engage the audience. Then I have to listen to determine if the participants 'got it.' If they didn't get it, I have to find a way to meet them where they are, use examples that are meaningful to them, and work with them until they understand. It's as much about listening as it is about talking."

—Sharon Mitchell, VP R&D Procter & Gamble, 2004

Here are a few more active learning methods that tend to work well for leader-teachers, and that can be adapted for many content areas and cultures around the world. For more on learning methods, see chapter 7 of *Leaders as Teachers* (Betof, 2009).

Skillful Questioning

Great questions engage participants. Bad questions have the opposite effect. Help leader-teachers plan some of their questions in advance. Open-ended questions help stimulate thinking, provided the questions are framed narrowly on the topic. For example, "What do you think?" is too open, whereas "What do you think about the action proposed and the chances that this action will deliver on the goal?" is much more focused. Help leader-teachers focus questions on the learning goals, not content details. Encourage leader-teachers to be comfortable with silence while the participants formulate a reasonable response. This thinking time may take 20 seconds or more.

Problem Solving

We are not talking about a simple math problem; rather, we are referring to setting out a situation that asks the participants to determine how to apply best practices, methods, or procedures to come up with a solution. The leader-teacher can bring a sense of real-life to the problem with simple comments such as, "I have personally seen this problem at three of our locations," or "I've had several people come to me for advice on issues like these." During the debrief, it is crucial for leader-teachers to clarify what responses are right and wrong, and those that could be taken to a higher level of sophistication.

Interactive Online Teaching

This method is ideal for multi-site companies and 24/7 cultures. By joining online discussions and leading dialogs in synchronous virtual classes, leaders can get insights into how individuals and entire teams are analyzing problems, considering options, and suggesting and collaborating on solutions. By posing thoughtful follow-up questions and comments, leader-teachers can help to inspire deeper thinking, and ensure their teams have the knowledge and skills for the job ahead.

Unique Leadership Perspective

Real stories told by leaders about their own experiences and beliefs can keep participants highly engaged because we are wired to remember and learn from stories. Whenever possible, encourage leader-teachers to develop their own **unique leadership perspective** (ULP), a story about their own beliefs and experiences that models what they expect from their organizations and from themselves. ULPs can be learning programs or part of a larger program.

You can help leader-teachers develop ULPs that have "head and heart impact" by using one of the story-starters that we categorize into four groups: topical areas, interview responses, meaningful quotes, and visual metaphors. See the Active Teaching Frame at the end of this chapter for an example of how to teach ULP development to a group.

Science Notes

Telling a story is different from talking about something. Storytelling engages at an emotional level. While business people often strive for logic as opposed to emotion, it is the emotional element that makes the content memorable. Emotional content is tagged in the brain with dopamine, the "feel good" neurotransmitter. This use of emotion is the equivalent of the brain's adding a sticky note "remember this!"

Topical Areas

Start by asking leader-teachers to consider a topic and write down or tell you their perspective. Some possible topics are listed in Figure 4.2. Then, help trigger new thoughts by going through the table of contents of related books with the leader-teacher. For example, on the topic of careers, ask about a significant career step. To trigger new thoughts talk through the part titles of the book *Just Promoted!*—"Establishing Yourself in Your New Role," "Achieving an Impact on the Organization," and "Managing the Impact of Moving Up on Your Family and Personal Life."

Figure 4.2: Topics to Draw Out Unique Leadership Perspectives

- Your success and failures throughout life and career
- Your role models
- Significant, possibly life-changing, events or turning points you have experienced
- Your beliefs about:
  - business growth, purpose, vision, and legacy
  - team work
  - innovation
  - disciplined execution
  - talent management and leadership development
  - decision-making, judgment calls, and courage
  - drive and work ethic
  - integrating fierce resolve and personal humility.

Interview Responses

With this story-starter method, interview leaders and have them respond to some of the following sentence starters. Help them expand on the answers by asking them to tell anecdotes and stories from their past as part of their responses.

- What I value most . . .
- What I deeply believe . . .
- Moments of truth and what I learned from them . . .
- Turning points in my life . . .
- My legacy . . . what I want to leave behind
- My leadership platform . . .
- The best advice/feedback I ever received, and how I used it . . .

Meaningful Quotes

Ask leaders to consider famous or meaningful quotes and describe why the quote has personal meaning for the leader. (This can also be accomplished with popular fables.) These discussions will often lead to stories that help leaders describe what is truly important to them. It's more than just the quote itself; it is also about the story behind the quote. Here are few of our favorites:

- "Talk does not cook rice," Chinese proverb
- "Good is the enemy of great," Jim Collins
- "Three people can keep a secret if two are dead," Benjamin Franklin
- "The conductor doesn't make a sound. The power of the conductor is derived from making other people feel powerful," Ben Zander, Boston Philharmonic Conductor

Visual Metaphors

A fourth way to help leaders develop and share their unique leadership perspectives through stories is through the use of visual images or metaphors. There are thousands of images on the web that could be selected to serve as the basis of a meaningful story. Many images can also be found at home or in the office in the form of pictures, physical objects, awards, newspaper headlines, magazine articles, and the like.

One leader used three hand drawn images to kick off the opening session with her leadership team shortly after being promoted. One image was a stick figure of a person. The second was a set of three over-lapping circles in the form of a Venn diagram. The third image was an arrow pointing up.

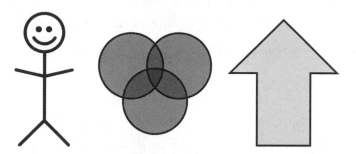

These story-starters begin the process. The rest is simply honing the story so that it can be told succinctly, using words and phrases that capture the listeners' attention. Encourage your leader-teachers to tell their stories in many settings over a period of four to six weeks, observing what phrases and words feel right and which get a head nod or other response.

Visuals for Enhanced Recall

Leader-teachers come into a learning event with the intent to convey a message and information. They probably come with their "visuals," which are all too often a set of text-heavy slides. Many business leaders could benefit from shifting the text into visuals that include images, graphics, and illustrations.

A common method for creating a business presentation is to capture the key points in bullets on a PowerPoint slide. These slides then become the script for the presenter. When this approach is used for learning programs, however, the leader-teacher ends up presenting a set of slides, rather than engaging interactively with participants.

To make the program more interactive, move the majority of the text to a separate notes page or Leader Guide. Then replace the text with visuals or fewer words, with a goal of no more than six lines of text, with no more than six words per line, on each slide. Challenge yourself and your leader-teachers to achieve a stretch goal of three by three.

It is easier to start with a visual approach rather than trying to add visuals to an existing set of materials. You can start the visual design process by asking the leader-teacher questions like, "If you had only one slide to talk off of for one hour, what model or image would we show on that slide?" or "Can we create a model that demonstrates the thought process you go through when you do this type of work?"

As with most things in life, finding the right balance between text and visuals is important. Use Figure 4.4 to help you determine how visual your learning materials are. Consider sharing Figure 4.4 with leader-teachers so they can shift their existing materials to a more visual approach on their own. It may seem counterintuitive, but this shift to visuals can help leader-teachers be more engaged with the participants and less nervous about being a trainer.

 Learn By Doing: How Visual Are Your Visuals?

Using learning materials you have on hand, classify the types of visuals that are used.

- ☐ Type 1: Read it (all text).
- ☐ Type 2: Emphasize it (all text).
- ☐ Type 3: Organize it (mix of text and graphics).
- ☐ Type 4: Label it (mix of text and graphics).
- ☐ Type 5: Visualize it (all visual).

If you were to estimate, what percentage of the materials are Type 3, 4, and 5? _____

A good goal is 80 percent with some type of visual.

Figure 4.4: Text-to-Visual Continuum

Text to Visual Continuum

Type 1
Read It
(all text)

Social Collaborative Learning

- Formal or Informal; Networked or Alone
- Four Tiers of Social Learning
  - Self-Paced E-Learning
  - Guided, Paced Cohort
  - Web Search
  - Community of Practice

Type 2
Emphasize It
(all text)

Social Collaborative Learning

- 4 Tiers
  - Individual
  - Cohort
  - Web Search
  - Community of Practice

Type 3
Organize It
(mix 1)

Social Collaborative Learning

Self-Paced E-Learning	Guided, Paced Cohort
Web Search	Community of Practice

Formality →

Networked →

Type 4
Label It
(mix 2)

Social Collaborative Learning

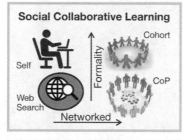

Self
Web Search
Cohort
CoP
Formality
Networked

Type 5
Visualize It
(all visual)

Social Collaborative Learning

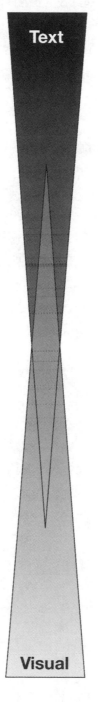

Text

Visual

© LaTAG, Owens 2013
Adapted from Visual Literacy,
(Moore & Dwyer, 1994) credited
to Wiseman's Typology.
(Wiseman, 1993, p. 19)

One of the strongest uses of visuals for leader-teachers is the use of images that embody their ULP, as described earlier in this chapter. Images that convey the heart of their story are most helpful.

Regardless of what type of visuals are added to your LAT-supported learning events, we encourage you to trend to the visual end of the text-to-visual continuum to improve learner retention as well as leader-teacher engagement.

 Quick Tip

When leader-teachers ask for more text on a screen, gently remind them:

- Visuals are a learner-aid, not the trainer script.
- As a leader-teacher, you are delivering a message, not a set of slides.
- If participants need to reference that much content, perhaps we should provide a handout.

Your Turn

Jot down your thoughts on the following topics.

What active teaching frames and active learning methods can you use immediately? Which would you like to introduce into future LAT programs? How might you do this?

_____

_____

What help do you think leader-teachers will need in order to develop their ULPs (unique leadership perspectives)? Where might ULPs be used to enhance LAT programs and curriculum?

_____

_____

How might you increase the use of visuals in LAT learning program? Are there any goals you could set to encourage an optimum balance of text and visuals in learning materials?

_____

_____

What cultural aspects of your workplace might inhibit the use of active teaching frames, ULPs or increased use of visuals? What might you do to mitigate these cultural elements?

_____

_____

Active Teaching Frame Examples

Figures 4.5 and 4.6 are two additional examples of active teaching frames filled with active learning methods.

Figure 4.5: Completed Active Teaching Design Template #2
Title of Training: Leading Diverse Teams **Frame:** Simulation/Debrief **Active Learning methods:** a. Simulation of a team working collaboratively to deliver a project b. Debrief
Description: One of the leader-teachers introduces the activity to the mid-level manager participants using the PAL method. **Purpose:** Practice the team collaboration skills as described in the pre-work video. **Agenda:** Build a structure based on a single word given to their team leader (joy, youth, collaboration, and success). Each of the five teams is given a different set of building materials. Plan the task and have the team leader get the plan approved by the general manager (leader-teacher) before beginning to build the structure. Then build the structure and have the group vote for their favorites during the debrief. **Limits:** The time frame is provided, and only materials found at the venue may be used. Team leaders share the plan with the leader-teacher, who adds a requirement to each one (for example, make it more circular or add some kind of sound to the construct, or add an element of height). Team leaders take the new requirements back to the team and construction begins. Halfway through the construction time the leader-teacher calls for attention and asks for a huddle of the team leaders. She explains that funding has been cut and that two teams have to be disbanded. Team leaders draw straws to determine who is out. Construction continues until time is up. The debrief begins by having the entire class walk around to each table to see what was built, after which the leader-teacher makes some observations and comments before going to the next table. Using the "applause meter," the class votes on their favorite, and that team wins first place in the buffet line for dinner.

Leader-Teacher Interaction:

The pair of leader-teachers are the key to making this meaningful. The leader-teachers point out the real-life corollaries to the need to get pre-approval, the addition of new requirements to the project, and cuts to funds and projects. During the activity, the leader-teachers circulate and listen in on conflicts, leaders who take charge without listening, how quickly disbanded teams (and their building materials) are integrated into other teams (or not), emotional responses, and so on. During the debrief, the leader-teachers listen to the presentations and then ask questions, point out their general observations (without putting down individuals), praise collaboration, and good use of team principles such as inclusiveness and use of diverse skills. Throughout the hour-long debrief, the leader-teachers make links to the workplace through comments and short stories.

Note that this one activity was proven to have a lasting impact on the individuals, even years later, as demonstrated in a research report published online by the Greater Cincinnati chapter of ASTD.

Figure 4.6: Completed Active Training Design Template #3

This example is about developing and communicating a unique leadership perspective. A ULP reflects the essence of what a leader believes, acts upon, models, teaches, and expects from herself and others in the organization. While ULPs are apparent in leaders' day-to-day actions, decisions, and communications, ULPs often come to life in the form of stories, anecdotes, and career reflections that have a personal and authentic feel.

Title of Training: Communicate Your Unique Leadership Perspective (ULP) Through Stories

Frame: Three-Level Program Design

Active Learning Methods: Many are used and identified within the description

a. Purposeful reading	f. Lager group share-out
b. Mini-lecture	g. Sentence completion
c. Small group task	h. Expanded sharing
d. Personal reflection	i. Action plan commitment
e. Peer teaching	

Description:

What: Theory, Concepts, Facts
- **Purposeful reading** by participants before the learning event, with the intent of being able to eventually create one's own leadership story:
  - chapter 1 of *The Leadership Challenge* (Kouzes and Posner 2012)
  - chapter 7, storytelling section of *Leaders as Teachers* (Betof 2009).

- **Mini-lecture** by the leader-teacher on the value and use of leadership storytelling. Participants intentionally refresh their thinking on the topic, in preparation for developing their own ULP. Subsequently, the participants will later be able to help leaders develop an ULP as part of their role as learning professionals.
- **Small group task,** for groups of three or four, to discuss the handout called "story-starters," specifically, how these might be used to convey one's ULP. Participants answer the question, "Do you have a preference for one set of story-starters?" Story starters list includes (a) topical areas, (b) interview responses, (c) meaningful quotes, and (d) visual metaphors.
- **Large group sharing** and debrief during which the leader-teacher facilitates a large group discussion that focuses on reinforcing key concepts and clarifying any questions about the importance and possible uses of story-starters in helping leaders to formulate ways to share their ULP.

So What: Personal Inquiry

- **Personal reflection** by participants making notes in their personal learning journal, with starter questions such as "Which of the above story starters might best help me to formulate my unique leadership perspective?" and "Which tie to our business or team challenges?"
- **Sentence completion** by participants to encourage deeper processing of the content by completing one or more of the following sentence stems: I learned . . . . , I re-learned . . . . , I was surprised . . . . , I realized . . . . , I could apply . . . . , I commit to . . . . , or you can count on me to . . . .
- **Peer teaching** by sharing one or two reflections within the same small group.
- **Large group sharing** with the leader-teacher using a "whip around the class" in which participants take turns to quickly state an opportunity they see for themselves that is a result of their thinking in the earlier steps. To build a "safe" environment, sharing is brief, with no elaboration.

Now What: Professional Application

- **Expanding sharing:** individuals > pairs > small groups > large group. In this part of the learning event, participants select their own ULP and share it using any of the story-starting methods, first in pairs and then in small groups. Then a few volunteers to share in the large group. Peers and leader-teachers provide feedback throughout this "Now what?" multi-step active learning process.
- **Action plan commitment** is documented by each participant. They set out a set of actions to implement, based on what they have learned. As part of the commitment, participants set dates by which they will apply this learning.

Chapter 5

Teach in the Moment

*"Things turn out best for the people who
make the best of the way things turn out."*

—John Wooden, educator, philosopher, and
successful men's college basketball coach

■ ■ ■

 Find Your Answers

This chapter helps you recognize and prepare opportunities to informally, yet powerfully,
teach every day. We call this **teaching in the moment**. As you read, think about your
answers to these questions:

- How can you best inventory opportunities to be more effective at
  teaching in the moment?
- How can you effectively plan teaching moments so that others
  can benefit?
- How can you help others regularly reflect and learn from their
  experiences?

Individuals, teams, and larger parts of the organization can each benefit and
learn if leaders take advantage of the many planned and unplanned teaching
moments that so frequently occur on a daily and weekly basis in your work setting.
We call this powerful, everyday teaching method teach in the moment. Every
leader can capitalize on learning opportunities by using this approach. Teaching

in the moment is an informal and potent way to help others learn immediately or shortly after a work experience. In this chapter, we will demonstrate how you can teach your leaders to be successful at teaching in the moment.

Examples of Teach in the Moment

As you read these examples, think about how you can encourage similar instances to happen more regularly throughout your organization, whether you are the leader doing it, or helping others to teach in the moment.

The Coach

Six healthcare company executives had been meeting for hours to determine the best course of action for a very promising and profitable product. The drug was a significant breakthrough for a medical condition that had no effective treatment. The FDA had approved the drug based on multi-year clinical trial results, but some safety issues had just been identified in the marketplace. It was unclear if the issues were real or just a statistical anomaly. The executives were trying to determine what to do. Should they pull the product off the market voluntarily? Conduct additional multi-year testing? While millions of dollars were at risk, more importantly, lives were on the line—both the lives of patients denied the drug if it was pulled from the market, and those who took it if the risk turned out to be real instead of a statistical anomaly. This was a true ethical dilemma.

There was considerable hand wringing by the six executives. After three hours there was still no resolution. At that point, the president of the company entered the meeting room unannounced and listened without saying a word. After ten minutes, he rose and, just before leaving the room, he simply looked at each executive one at a time and said, "Make sure you do the right thing." The meeting was over twenty minutes later with a creative solution that ensured additional accelerated clinical testing, clear communication with the FDA, and a plan to maintain availability of the product for patients who needed it.

More than 20 years later, the leaders involved still talk about the powerful ethical lesson they learned from their president, whose nickname had been established years before by his direct reports. Today, well into his 80s, he remains The

Coach. He is a principled and results-oriented leader who always set the ethical tone at the top. He also is a master at teaching in the moment.

Pat's Meeting Debriefs

Pat always saves approximately 10 minutes at the end of every meeting she leads to conduct a concise three question meeting debrief. Pat's top values include strong teamwork, learning from everything she and her team does, and continuous improvement. She models these three values each time she debriefs a team meeting. Here are the questions Pat uses to conduct her learning debriefs:

- What did we do well during the meeting and how well did we adhere to our agreed-to behavioral Rules of Engagement?
- What did not go well during the meeting and might be inconsistent with our behavioral Rules of Engagement?
- What is at least one thing that we can commit to doing better at our next meeting?

Throughout the day Pat regularly teaches in the moment. She realizes the value it adds to those involved and to her team as a whole. Her meeting debriefs are an example of her dedication and skill in this regard.

Steve's Learning Discussions

Steve, VP of marketing at a consumer products company, always leaves with his direct reports after they have made a marketing presentation. He reserves 30 minutes to an hour ahead of time to meet with each individual who made the presentation. During the meeting they discuss what went well and what did not go well and extract learning from the presentation experience that can be applied in similar settings. Steve specifically calls these "learning discussions." He never misses the opportunity to augment the discussion and presenter's self-evaluation with his own insightful observations and suggestions for improvements or alternative ways of addressing the topic. Steve is an example of a leader who can teach in the moment.

An Argument

During a team meeting, long-simmering differences between four members of the team unexpectedly surfaced in the form of a full-throated argument. Those not involved were startled, even shocked. Aretha, the team leader, was caught off guard because she had not known of the disagreements between several team members. While surprised at how loud, quickly, and publically the argument surfaced, Aretha kept her composure. An unplanned teaching moment was at hand. She turned a very uncomfortable situation into an impressive in the moment teaching and learning opportunity.

Aretha had recently completed a company leadership program where she learned about emotional intelligence and how the limbic system of the brain can easily hijack reason and common sense. She asked everyone to clear their schedules for the next two hours and called a 20-minute time-out so everyone could cool down. When the team re-entered the room, Aretha skillfully facilitated a no-lose, conflict resolution session using skills she had learned at a class on parenting teenagers. An hour and a half later, several important issues had been settled. Agreements were decided. Follow-up actions were confirmed by each team member. As the team left the room, one woman who was involved in the argument broke the tension. She joked, asking if she could take Aretha home with her to work on her teenagers. A lot of learning and modeling of desired leadership behaviors took place during this extended two hour meeting and unplanned teaching moment.

 Science Notes

Our brains contain mirror neurons. Our mirror neurons perform a virtual reality simulation in our minds that mimics what we see others doing. Some believe mirror neurons may represent the neurophysiologic equivalent of empathy. When a mentor and mentee interact, more happens than simple dialog. The people unconsciously mimic each other in multiple ways, building a stronger bond between them.

Walk 'n Talks

Mike likes to tap into his team members' thinking on a regular basis. He also believes that a little exercise is healthy for everyone. Three times a week, Mike has an open invitation for team members who are available to join him for what he has termed 45-minute walk 'n talks. During these free-flowing discussions while they stroll about the campus, Mike rarely misses the opportunity to raise timely topics and answer questions. He frequently brings up topics that are hard to discuss when people are sitting in an office or meeting room. Some walk 'n talk topics are planned and others just happen. Everyone agrees the discussions are valuable. There is a lot of teaching and learning, and breaking up a long day with a walk is both healthy and helpful for everyone.

Teaching in the Hallways

Joan prides herself on taking advantage of just about every opportunity for learning to occur. She is famous in her company for how much she can discuss, analyze, and teach in a three to five minute period going from meeting to meeting in the spacious hallways of her company. People say traveling with her from one meeting to another is a learning laboratory. Joan teaches throughout the day and those around her benefit as they learn and gain new insights.

Teaching in Town Hall Meetings

One CEO we know estimates he teaches 10 to 20 different mini-lessons during each 90-minute town meeting he conducts. His 20 minutes of planned comments are loaded with valuable information he wants to share. He then fields 10 to 15 questions. The CEO takes advantage of every question to teach and emphasize particular points. He makes it easy to ask difficult or sensitive questions so he can share information that often is not easy to discuss. Humor, candor, and enthusiastic responses are constant assets. The CEO is very conscious of being a role model and hopes that these behaviors rub off on others. He encourages other leaders to conduct similar town meetings in many company locations.

Now that we have looked at the examples, let's take a look at how you personally take advantage of in the moment teaching opportunities.

Learning From Leader-Teachers

"One of the most powerful methods of teaching as a leader is to provide 'teachable moments' in the daily process of running our business. I remember when one of my directors was getting feedback from a peer in a meeting and replied, 'I 100 percent disagree with your feedback on all counts.' His reply shocked the team and sucked all the air right out of the room. I suggested we move on to the next topic and at the end of the meeting used the opportunity to pull him aside and coach that a better response might have been, 'What are you trying to improve with your feedback? I would appreciate a chance to speak with you in greater detail after the meeting.' After my coaching, he realized that his comments had disrupted the meeting and also shut down the other person, and likely any future feedback, which could have been used to strengthen a strained relationship. While classroom development on giving and receiving feedback is useful, this teachable moment is much more powerful and is more likely to truly change behavior."

—Jay Glasscock, Vice President/General Manager, Thermo Fisher

Teach in the Moment Opportunities

Each example in the previous section demonstrates the power of teaching in the moment. Opportunities such as these are all around us every day. To help you spot them, we've categorized some common goals and typical situations for teaching in the moment in Figure 5.1. Read through the lists, then look back through the examples to see if you can spot the categories into which each falls.

Figure 5.1: Teach in the Moment Sample Categories	
Goal Categories for Teach in the Moment	**Situation Categories for Teach in the Moment**
• Broaden perspective with stories or questions • Keep the goal foremost in their minds • Reinforce values and principles • Role model a principle or practice • Seed ideas and thoughts • Shape a strategic plan • Start a major department, unit, or team initiative • Other: _____	• Beginning or wrapping-up a task or project • Making difficult decisions • Dealing with everyday interactions and events • Managing planned events • Brainstorming or dealing with conflict • Addressing unexpected emergencies • Sharing a unique leadership perspective • Conducting just-in-time or on-the-job training • Other: _____

Learn By Doing:
Teach in the Moment Opportunity Search

This activity is designed to help you plan to increase your own use of the teach in the moment method. Try it yourself, step by step. Consider using this activity to help other leaders in your organization expand their use of teaching in the moment opportunities.

Step 1: Find last week's teach in the moment opportunities. Have your calendar handy. Look at your last five days of work. List below, up to 10 planned and unplanned teachable moments that you took advantage of during this period.

- Describe your teach in the moment opportunity.
- Note if the opportunity was planned (P) or unplanned (U).
- Note if the opportunity was with an individual (I) or in a group/team setting (G).
- What goal was, or could have been, accomplished? (See Figure 5.1 for examples.)
- What was the situation? (See Figure 5.1 for examples.)

Description	P or U	I or G	Goal	Situation
1.				
2.				
3.				
4.				
5.				
6.				
7.				
8.				
9.				
10.				

Step 2: Find last week's missed opportunities. List up to five teach in the moment opportunities you believe you missed over the past five days.

1. _____

_____

2. _____

_____

3. _____

_____

4. _____

_____

5. _____

_____

Step 3: Find the patterns. As you look at the opportunities—both used and missed—do you notice any patterns? Is there something you can do to take advantage of more of these opportunities? Jot your thoughts here.

_____

_____

_____

Step 4: Find future opportunities. Look at your work calendar for the next week. List at least five opportunities that you can anticipate and plan to teach in the moment during this period. Place an * next to each opportunity for which you know you will take action.

1. _____

   _____

2. _____

   _____

3. _____

   _____

4. _____

   _____

5. _____

   _____

Are there other opportunities?

_____

Step 5: Reflect on teach in the moment opportunities. As a way to reflect on the possible value, and to personalize information inventoried through this activity, please take a few moments to review this entire activity. Please complete at least two or three of the following unfinished sentence stems as a way to summarize your thoughts.

- I learned . . .

- I re-learned . . .

- I realized . . .

- I was surprised . . .

- I wonder . . .

- I hope . . .

- You can count on me to . . .

This Teach in the Moment Opportunity Search is designed to help leaders understand and take action on both the planned and unplanned teaching moments that occur on a weekly basis in a typical leadership work setting. Steps 1 to 5 also serve as another example of the "what," "so what," and "now what" active learning model described in chapter 4.

Teaching Tips to Help Others Reflect and Learn From Their Experiences

Purposeful reflection is another powerful learning device. When leaders encourage and role model purposeful reflections, learning is more likely to be remembered and re-applied. Many professionals and leaders do not know how to take full advantage or do not take the time to make sense of what they have experienced or are experiencing. These are usually lost learning opportunities.

Leader-teachers have tremendous opportunities to help others learn more effectively from their experience. In particular, planned and unplanned teaching moments are rich reservoirs of professional learning and personal insight. A key to these robust learning opportunities is the reflection phase of the teaching-learning process.

 Insights From Learning Professionals

"Mentoring and coaching are important parts of a leader's job," says Mike Kelly, VP of L&D at Macy's credit and customer services. "But you know, I can't be there with my employees all the time, so I tell my people what I have learned from Jim Rohn, a great author and speaker: 'Work harder on yourself than you do on your job' and 'Your success on the job is determined by what you do off the job.'" This is a simple example of how Mike teaches in the moment.

Reflective learning is an active process of critically analyzing events and experiences to uncover underlying lessons, information, and insights about oneself.

Reflection can provide perspective on your past experiences as well as your current work and life circumstances. This is especially true of an event that has just happened or is ongoing. We also know from research that there is a relationship between a leader's ability and willingness to reflect deeply on their experiences and the amount of personal and professional learning that occurs.

Here are some developmental benefits of reflection:

- provides meaning to an experience
- helps the learner to gain perspective or new perspective on an opportunity or challenge
- provides opportunities to look at alternatives and consequences of actions
- helps to challenge your thinking and beliefs about situations, problems, and opportunities
- improves your ability to self-assess your capabilities
- helps a person to see situations from other's points of view
- facilitates transfer of learning from unfamiliar situations to one's own context.

While experienced leader-teachers listen more than they talk, during a reflection, they make extensive use of questions, make comments, and provide feedback at just the right time. The following are some examples of practices and questions that leader-teachers can use to facilitate reflection during and after teaching moments:

- Ask this series of questions: What was supposed to happen? What actually happened? What would you do differently if you did this again?
- What did you learn from the experience? Is there anything you may have missed or learned completely during the experience?
- Were there professional or personal insights you gained from the experience?
- What did you think was happening? Did you check to make sure?
- What are the intended and possible unintended consequences of your thinking or taking the action you are considering?
- What might have happened if you . . . ?
- Was there something that prompted you to . . . ?

- If you look at this situation next year, do you think you will see it the same way?
- Are there any other actions you could have taken?
- If you were coaching or mentoring someone in this situation, what would you say?
- What surprised you about this situation?
- Given what you know, are there other ways of approaching this situation?
- What was easiest for you? Hardest for you?
- How does this fit into your current priorities? Are there adjustments you might make?

 Learning From Leader-Teachers

"Leaders as teachers is a life skill for managing. LAT is the backbone for all my management interactions. I use this skill subconsciously now, and I teach it to others as I network, conduct peer reviews, and in my daily management. It has proven to be effective in every culture, wherever in the world I travel."

—Bruce Stanley, formerly Sr. Director, Contracting Operations, BD, now Principal of the Stanley East Consulting Group

Be Prepared

It is not difficult to take advantage of more teaching in the moment opportunities. It does help to be prepared. Preparation comes from learning to recognize the moments, checking your calendar for possible upcoming opportunities, having your own **unique leadership perspectives** (see chapter 4), and practicing and honing skills to draw out learning from experiences.

Your Turn

Jot down your thoughts on the following topics:

What are the best ways to use the inventory of your own opportunities to more effectively teach in the moment?

_____

_____

What are the three to five best practices or questions for you that can help others to effectively use reflection during learning opportunities? What is a situation during the next week when you could use one or more of these?

_____

_____

Harness the Power of Collaborative Learning

"The way to get good ideas is to get lots of ideas, and throw the bad ones away."

—Linus Pauling

∎∎∎

 ## Find Your Answers

Social learning is not an education fad, or a method for crowdsourcing ideas. We now understand that much of learning is social. In this chapter, you will learn how leader-teachers can encourage a social learning environment to yield its benefits. As you read, think about your answers to these questions:

- How might you adapt current learning programs to act more like "learning laboratories" where leaders and teams encounter presentations, content, activities, and an environment that is designed to help them come together to conquer challenges, opportunities, and problems?
- How can leader-teachers help you shape learning programs around the real challenges confronting people, and help you embed learning into work?
- How can leader-teachers influence your organization to frame business problems as learning needs; recast failures as learning opportunities; and adapt strategies, plans, and tactics as lessons emerge from experiences in the field?

Our increasingly complex business world demands new learning approaches, such as social collaborative learning, to help organizations discover the best paths forward, and to investigate what will and won't work in a marketplace characterized by constant change. For many years, traditional learning has been one-directional: from teachers to students, experts to employees. However, the complexity of today's world narrows the scope of knowledge that any single teacher or expert can master and maintain. Business conditions are sometimes so new and novel that experts have yet to develop methods and approaches that can put an organization on a path to success. If there are known methods, they might work in some regions and not in others. Leaders and teams often find themselves facing an overwhelming flood of information that leads to a sea of possible paths to execute the company's strategy. As businesses confront an exponential rate of change, they must learn just enough to confidently take their first steps into the marketplace, and then continue to learn and adapt as they discover what is working and what is not. The competitive clock no longer affords time to perfect an approach before making a move. How can leaders and teams carefully test possibilities, learning as they go, only fully committing to the option with the greatest potential for success?

This is where the social nature of learning delivers great value as people learn from each other, scaffolding ideas one onto another, and building higher levels of understanding. The best results come from dynamic interactions among academics, leaders, domain experts, peers, customers, and partners all working together to construct meaning as marketplace conditions and consumer preferences change.

Social learning offers an answer by creating environments that behave like "learning laboratories," where **leader-teachers** share wisdom, design experiments, lead dialogs, pressure-test theories, and exert tension for change. L&D professionals should feel the same time pressures about adopting social learning as their functional colleagues do in pursuing clues about the next industry trend and the unmet needs tugging at customer loyalty.

Characterizing the Social Learning Environment

Learning can be formal or informal; it can be done alone, or in a group or network as illustrated in Figure 6.1a.

Figure 6.1: Connectivity of the Social Learning Environment

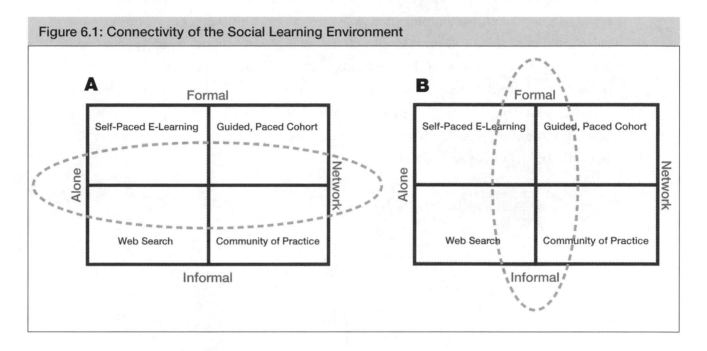

Learners have two options when going it alone. On the informal side, self-starting learners do the best they can to fill knowledge gaps by searching for answers and insights on the Internet. The problem with this approach is that there's very little support to check the validity of what they're finding and learning, and even less chance that different employees will fall into standardized ways of working, leading to confusing interactions with customers.

On the formal side, employees engage in self-paced e-learning that has been vetted by experts, but that often fails to deeply engage learners, resulting in low completion rates.

Academics studying the issue of high dropout rates in traditional e-learning programs found three main causes: student dissatisfaction, irrelevant learning materials, and lack of return on investment. A study assessing completion rates for e-learning showed that when participants were assigned courses through a corporate LMS, without formal notification (self-enrollment), only 9 percent of employees started courses and 6 percent completed them. When the learning function formally assigned courses and gave appropriate notifications, 22 percent of the participants started the course and 13 percent completed it. Start and completion rates increased significantly in this study after special programs and marketing activities (the study's APCP Methods) were developed to make learning content relevant to the employees' jobs (Tufan 2010).

Figure 6.2: E-Learning Start and Completion Rates

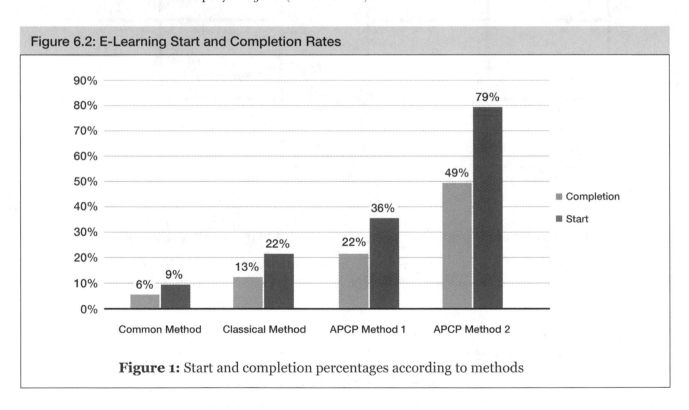

Figure 1: Start and completion percentages according to methods

One approach for developing new knowledge and teasing out effective practices on the network side of the quadrant finds people joining communities of practice in their areas of professional interest. Network members usually do a good job of curating and validating information, but participants are left to construct their own learning paths.

Finally, the formal, networked approach to learning in the upper right quadrant of Figure 6.1b is where social learning models reside. Social, collaborative learning is accomplished by incorporating synchronous and asynchronous exchanges where individuals bring their wisdom and experience to bear on course content.

 Quick Tip

Be nearly right in your social learning designs, and then get moving; get people learning from each other as soon as possible. Learn to feel comfortable taking your first steps, knowing you'll adjust the social learning environment as you discover what works best for your leaders and teams in your company's culture.

The Guided Learning Journey: A Best Practice Approach to Social Learning

In Figure 6.1, the social learning example noted in the upper right quadrant is called a **guided learning journey** (GLJ). One reason the GLJ appeals to many large organizations is because it lets them build collaborative, networked learning experiences for large populations of leaders and employees, with much greater convenience than most traditional learning approaches offer. But early adopters are finding that when GLJs are designed well, added convenience and reduced cost are the more minor benefits. The real value comes by helping organized cohorts design and implement action plans as part of the learning experience.

GLJs earn their name because they have the following characteristics:

- The GLJ represents a journey that never ends, but that is managed from the point when participants confront a business challenge that requires mastering new knowledge and information, through to a future of continued practice.

- The GLJ is led by guides, rather than the traditional teacher. The guide responsibility shifts from faculty to moderators to leaders to participants themselves.
- The formal learning part of the GLJ spans a period of weeks, although the work required of participants remains the same as that expected in a two- or three-day workshop. The delivery of content is stretched out so that participants have more time to discuss and reflect on what they are learning, especially as they encounter moments on the job that add new meaning and context to the ideas they are learning.

Critical Success Factors for Social Learning

Effective social learning embeds learning into work and rapidly focuses learners on the "how to do it" versus the traditional "what to do." It's about doing versus knowing. Effective social learning creates an environment that lets people work directly on job objectives with all the support to help them achieve the best possible results. The course material may introduce theories and hypothetical case examples early on, but quickly shifts to learning activities shaped around the actual challenges participants are facing in their jobs.

Social learning programs must consider much more than "what" people need to learn. The "what" represents information compressed and abstracted from experts so that it can be more easily distributed to learners. The fast pace of business demands that learners quickly get to the "how" of what they're learning. The "how" represents more specific information. Leader-teachers can be immensely helpful here by suggesting possible starting points and ways to move forward through the mass of information available to everyone through today's technology.

Effective social learning programs do the following things well:

- support the distribution of knowledge across networks; including the interactions between people and resources
- offer ways for participants to adapt content and shape the approaches that are best suited to their local contexts
- provide access to a set of resources for deep immersion into the subject matter, and when needed, access to content that is related to the topic under consideration

- enable expert-to-peer, peer-to-peer, and peer-to-community learning, collaboration, knowledge capture, knowledge sharing, and understanding
- collect the successes and failures of practical field experience to accelerate learning curves for future cohorts.

The following table illustrates how activities and exercises in a social learning program move participants through a process of learning, understanding, and doing, while engaging with faculty, moderators, leader-teachers, and peers.

 ## Quick Tip: Planning the Steps of a Learning Journey

- **Watch** a well-produced, videotaped lecture or demonstration that evokes an emotional reaction (engaging introduction).
- **Read** a document that presents deeper analysis of the topic (content depth).
- **Breakout** into groups to share thoughts and conduct peer reviews (to examine and explore together).
- **Discuss** by getting all ideas on the table about how to proceed, and collectively suggest ways to overcome barriers (to contextualize).
- **Reflect** and help them consider what they are learning within the context of their jobs, and help them use ideas from discussions and breakout groups to begin to form plans describing how they'll apply what they've learned (to internalize).
- **Try it out,** by assigning ways to test new thinking in their actual environments (to experiment or practice).
- **Report back** and share lessons from the field, testing, and experiences (to synthesize).
- **Meet** to spend time together reviewing what they have learned so far, what they understand well, and if knowledge gaps still remain (to socialize lessons and application opportunities).

The Value of Leader-Teacher Participation in Social Learning

Now that you have a sense for the elements that make up social learning experiences, let's consider the role of leader-teachers in social learning and show how leader-teacher interactions might enhance such programs, through the example of a GLJ.

Help Shape Journeys Around Actual Work

There's a widening gap between theory and practice as work becomes more and more specialized and differentiated—by where people work, how fast their industries are changing, the types of technologies they use to do their jobs, and many other factors. So while academics and other experts can teach the concepts of analyzing big data to peer deeper into the behaviors of individual market segments, for example, they can't teach program participants exactly how to tailor products and messaging to compel customers to action. But leader-teachers can give us clues as to where teams are struggling to grow revenue, hit sales targets, or identify compelling product features. They can describe the types of work that must be improved to get better answers to business challenges, and then learning practitioners can craft the discussions, peer interactions, and work-related exercises to improve how they work.

Set the Tone and Challenge for the GLJ

Before a GLJ begins, leader-teachers can describe that point on the horizon that participants should aim for. Leader-teachers are in the same boat as all other experts. They can no longer offer a perfect description for a single path to success as they might have done in past eras. Instead, they must share a sense about the direction the group is heading, some of the kinds of obstacles the group is likely to come up against, and examples and reasons why past practices aren't likely to be effective. By presenting, either through videotaped lecture or live presentation in a virtual class, leader-teachers can describe the subject areas that participants should probe and explore, the speed at which teams must take action, and how participants should think about their initial steps when they do decide to take action.

Join Discussions

When participants address provocative questions in discussion activities embedded within a GLJ, all kinds of solutions and possibilities can emerge in addition to all varieties of challenges and concerns. As leader-teachers read discussion forum posts, they can determine if there's a shared mindset for "the big picture"—the positive business outcome the group should be aiming to achieve. This can help ensure that interactions aren't distracted by prior mistakes and trying to find someone to blame. Leader-teachers post discussion responses to interject higher-level perspectives, offer new information that was previously unavailable to the group, and broaden their view about organization capabilities to focus the dialogs on defined business outcomes.

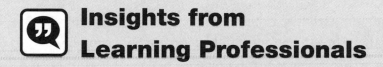

Insights from Learning Professionals

"While we in the talent organization are passionate about facilitating, we wanted to wean ourselves from doing all of it ourselves. So we made an offer to all of our certified facilitators that they could co-facilitate with one of us on any of the virtual courses we were doing in the last part of the calendar year. One of our facilitators, Cindy, director of radiology, wanted to enhance her training skills. She had already earned the LATC (leaders-as-teachers certification) in the live-in-person modality, but that's just the kind of person she is, always wanting to improve. So she and I taught a virtual class together. After our second virtual class, we did a little debrief, as we always do, and I asked her, 'So Cindy, how are you liking this virtual training?' And she said, 'Jerry, I am almost embarrassed to admit this, because I didn't think I ever wanted to teach virtually. But after seeing how this is done, after seeing how you can engage people who you can't see face-to-face, I've got to admit, I think I like this better than face-to-face. When I had taken virtual classes in the past, it was so boring, and I multitasked through it. But I now see that within 90 minutes, you not only accomplish so much with your participants, but you have them all engaged! Sign me up for more!'"

—Jerry Lewis, Director, Talent & Organizational Effectiveness, Banner Health

Provide Feedback on Individual Projects and Group Work Products

Leader-teachers are often asked to review the results of action learning. As cohorts develop solutions to address problems they've been assigned to carry out in an action-learning activity, leader-teachers ask questions about their proposed solutions, press their assumptions, and suggest things to consider as a follow-up to a review meeting. A GLJ presents the same kinds of opportunities, either in online posts or during live sessions, for leaders to review work as participants complete assignments within course. Leader-teachers also can share relevant examples from their own experiences with the topic at hand to help participants think deeper, or slightly differently, about the solutions they're pursuing.

Help Illustrate the "How"

When theories and ideas are presented as part of a course, it's sometimes hard for participants to think about how to get started. Leader-teachers can help enormously by describing how to break the concepts down to manageable chunks, and then sharing examples of the first few small steps to get started. This might just be enough to help people overcome the inertia of sticking to their familiar routines. Again, leader-teachers can share their suggestions through a videotaped lecture, a discussion post, or during a live, virtual class.

Collaborate With Faculty

Facilitators and moderators who serve as the main guides for a GLJ are paying close attention to the discussions, practice exercises, and breakout group projects taking place within the GLJ. These program guides can inform leader-teachers about promising ideas being developed by the group, new challenges being identified, or points that seem to be misunderstood. Leader-teachers can routinely check in with program guides, and help highlight original thinking or bold ideas. They might also recognize underlying issues that must be addressed in response to potential challenges being raised, or to clarify concepts that are causing confusion. Leader-teachers should consider themselves part of the team of guides who can help to adjust the group's journey as needed, and as the group moves toward its new understanding and new course of action to address the challenge.

Serve as a Facilitator or Guest Speaker in Virtual Classes

One natural role for leader-teachers is to facilitate one or more of the live, weekly virtual classes that are part of a GLJ. These sessions let participants talk directly with faculty and other program guides to ask questions, have learning points clarified, and present the results of activities they've completed during the week. Leader-teachers can use these weekly sessions to engage directly with participants to address the ideas and points raised in discussion forums and to comment on progress or the nature of the work participants are demonstrating as they complete activities and lessons. Remember, a virtual session can be recorded on video or audio to let those who missed the live class hear the event as if they were there, and can also be used as an asset for future cohorts.

Support Field Experience

Once the formal part of a GLJ ends, an informal journey begins. This journey involves the ongoing practice, testing, and refining of ideas presented in the course as they are applied on the job, and as participants shape their approaches to their local contexts. Leader-teachers gain invaluable knowledge about the marketplace when they monitor the successes and failures of putting new ideas and solutions into action. This is when leaders learn from participants how they, as leaders, need to adapt the work of their teams to enable them to be even more successful in the current marketplace.

Consider How Leader-Teachers Would Support Your GLJ

Using the example in Figure 6.3 as a template, think about how you can modify a program you currently deliver to become a GLJ, and where you could engage your leader-teacher community to improve steps along the journey.

Figure 6.3: Example Outline for a Guided Learning Journey (GLJ)

This outlines a GLJ intended to help leaders review results of an annual employee engagement study, and plan actions to address the findings.

MODULE 1: Overview and Orientation
- READ: Welcome
- WATCH: Welcome Video
- ATTEND: Live Virtual Class
- READ: Course Objectives
- WRITE: Review and Complete Your Profile
- DISCUSS: Introduce Yourself and Meet Your Cohort

MODULE 2: Setting the Table: 2011, a Year in Review
- READ: Module Introduction
- READ: Current Employee Engagement Results
- READ: Employee Engagement Survey Executive Summary
- REFLECT: What Did You See in the Survey Results
- READ: An Engagement Refresher
- REFLECT: Thoughts About the Engagement Survey Now
- WATCH: A 2011 Survey Review
- DISCUSS: Lessons Learned from the Survey

MODULE 3: Connections, Intersections, and Overcoming the Narrative Impulse
- READ: Module Introduction
- READ: Why Connections Matter as We Build Engagement
- REFLECT: Initial Thoughts on Why Connections Matter
- READ: The Human Moment at Work
- REFLECT: Initial Thoughts on The Human Moment at Work
- WATCH: The Umbrella Man
- DISCUSS: Overcoming the Narrative Impulse

MODULE 4: Conference Workshop Session
- ATTEND: Live Workshop Session

Your Turn

Jot down your thoughts on the following questions.

As you think about the possibilities for integrating social collaborative learning in your LAT initiative, consider which technology-aided elements might augment current learning programs. Check off the ones you might use initially:

- ☐ Video-based lectures to support "flipped" classrooms where participants watch lectures on their own time, then come together (virtually or face-to-face) to discuss and apply
- ☐ Discussion forums
- ☐ Breakout group activities (online, synchronous or asynchronous)
- ☐ Virtual class meetings
- ☐ Online communities to support sharing experiences from the field and ongoing practice as a follow-up to formal learning
- ☐ Other social learning elements _____

_____

_____

Can you build practice exercises and support tools into current leadership development programs to help leader-teachers build new skills that will improve the value of social learning programs? (For example, leading effective dialogs and discussions to help groups develop shared understanding, use effective questioning to help pressure test ideas and expand participants' thinking, and practicing mentorship to encourage others when they are working to apply what they've learned.) Which programs and approaches are you considering?

_____

_____

Describe three ways that you might engage leader-teachers in your social learning programs. Which ways do you think are more suited to your current culture? Which will take more effort to introduce into your current culture?

_____

_____

_____

Chapter 7

Establish Your Brand to Drive Business Results and Learning

"We want to be a net exporter of talent throughout our company."

—A talent and development department head
describing the brand image of her function

■ ■ ■

 ## Find Your Answers

Leaders and learners choose to spend time and energy on those things that have brand equity that attracts them. This chapter guides you to develop and deliver brand equity for your LAT initiative that can capture the hearts and minds of your company's best and brightest. As you read, think about your answers to these questions:

- What is the character of your LAT brand? What do you want it to stand for?
- How do you create a brand logo? How will you know if your logo is good?
- How could you use the brand? Where could you use the brand logo?

How do you want people to view the organization's LAT-supported programs that you are designing? What image do you want to pop into their heads when they hear about it? That is what branding is all about. When we brand something, we embed meaning into it. In part, we do this by using a visual logo and a name to represent that meaning. If we do it well, when seen, the logo and name trigger something in people's brains causing them to unpack all that meaning in a single glance.

For example, what image pops into your head for Coca-Cola? McDonalds? Apple? Google? MasterCard? Consider how you feel about these brands. The makers of these brands hope that you get a positive feeling, maybe even an affinity with their brand, so that you want to use, buy, or engage with the brand. This is what you can achieve with a good LAT-connected brand within your company. The brand makes the emotional connection to people's wants and needs, and can capture the heart and engage the mind of your company's best and brightest—your **leader-teachers**. This chapter guides you to identify what you are branding, decide what your LAT-related brand stands for, add a visual brand logo, and put your brand out there for others to see. Build value into your brand, deliver on your brand's promise, and watch how many followers you will attract.

 Learning From Leader-Teachers

"The leaders as teachers concept elevates leadership training from conceptual to an experience that strengthens business performance and an organization's culture."

—Linda Michalopoulos, Senior HR Director, Clinton Health Access Initiative
(formerly, VP, HR Becton Dickinson)

What Will You Brand?

Your company has a brand that it shares externally. Let's call this brand the "parent" brand. Your LAT brand, if done well, will give a sense of being part of the family. There may be other brands within your company that are part of the family, such as your computer support system or department, or a program designed for work-life balance. They could be programs, groups, services, and products that are used internally. Study your organization's internal brands in order to guide you toward what appeals to your workforce and works within your culture.

Now consider what you are branding. Are you branding a learning organization? A set of training programs? A LAT approach? Perhaps your brand will represent the equivalent of the Good Housekeeping Seal of Approval or UL (Underwriters Laboratory) or even FDA-approved, all of which certify that a product meets certain standards, and gives consumers confidence about the quality of the product.

 ## Learn By Doing: What Are You Branding?

Explore what you could brand. Check those that are possible options for you.

- ☐ A brand that certifies that leader-teachers are involved and the quality is great.
- ☐ A corporate university that offers a series of colleges geared toward people by level, or function, or are based on a set of topics such as the organization's core competencies.
- ☐ A regular series of learning events based on a learning method or time slot, for example, a "lunch-and-learn" series, which prompts people to apply what they learned.
- ☐ A single-topic series of events or interventions, for example: quality or diversity.
- ☐ A strategic set of learning programs intended to accomplish a specific purpose, perhaps based on a new company initiative.
- ☐ A series of town hall meetings, perhaps with a different senior leader taking responsibility for leading each year.
- ☐ An annual learning event that reviews successes of the past year and helps employees connect their upcoming work to the next year's corporate strategy.
- ☐ Programs within the larger program. A corporate university may have its own distinct brand. Within the corporate university, there may be individual programs with unique brands that have a similar look-and-feel to indicate that it is clearly part of the larger family of programs.
- ☐ The leaders-as-teachers approach, itself, signaling to the organization that there is a set of programs that include leader-teacher involvement.
- ☐ Your learning and development organization and its services.

What Is Your Brand Personality and Brand Promise

Your LAT brand is neither the name of the program nor the logo or image that represents it. Your brand is more like a personality that promises something. To jumpstart your thinking about your LAT-related brand, consider these two well-known brands and their personalities and the promises these brands make.

Apple: "Apple's brand promise is 'we make it easier to love technology, so that you can experience the future.' . . . Apple is 'the brand for the smart, independent, informally classy person . . .'" (Robb 2013).

Mr. Clean: "The original model for the image of Mr. Clean was a United States Navy sailor from the city of Pensacola, Florida, although some people may think he is a genie based on his earring, folded arms, and tendency to appear magically at the appropriate time" (Mr. Clean 2013).

With these classic models for inspiration, read through the Brand Character and Promise Learn By Doing activity to guide you as you formulate the character and promise for your LAT brand. The results of your activity can be easily handed off to a graphic artist for translation into a brand logo or graphic, which we talk about later in this chapter. Feel free at any time to take a sneak peak at the two examples shown in Figure 7.1.

Learn By Doing: Brand Character and Promise

Step 1: Brainstorm Characteristics. Start by describing the character of your brand, writing down a list of descriptive adjectives. Use the types of words that you might use to describe a person. Make a long list of desirable traits. The first item is listed for you. Figure 7.1 shows a few more examples.

- _____Business-relevant_____
- _____
- _____
- _____
- _____
- _____
- _____
- _____
- _____
- _____

Step 2: Link it to the business. Because your LAT brand is linked to your business or organization, your next step is to identify which words above are a mismatch with the character of your business. You can either change the word or delete it. Now highlight words that are consistent with your company's or organization's image. As you consider your company's character, add any words that come to mind that fit both the company and your LAT-related brand.

Step 3: Speak to your target group. Now consider who you are talking to with your brand character words. The goal is for your target group—the potential leader-teachers and future learners—to feel attracted to your brand. Use a thesaurus and consider alternative words with different connotations that may have more appeal for your target. For example, fast-paced, is a great characteristic, but if the learning program is for a drug research group that works on long clinical drug trials, the term fast-paced is out-of-sync with their jobs. Instead, replace fast-paced with a word like energized to appeal to these smart people who quickly understand learning content and often want to move on to the next intellectual challenge. Adjust your choice of words to be in-sync with the language, communication patterns, and jobs of your target group. Now, having considered a broad range of possibilities, select three to five words that best characterize your LAT initiative and appeal to your target group.

List your top choices here:

- _____
- _____
- _____
- _____
- _____

Step 4: Consider what you are promising. The words you have chosen for your brand form the basis of a promise you are making to those who teach and those who learn within the programs under this brand name. Consider this: can you deliver on those promises? For example, if you desire a brand that is "cutting edge," yet are delivering programs about standard business practices, the mismatch will cause your brand to lose credibility. Instead, be realistic about what you can deliver and do it well. This might be a good time to review the Your Turn activity in chapter 2 where you jotted down notes about the scope of your LAT approach, business drivers, and structural elements. You may find that there is a disconnect. That's OK. Creating a brand is a creative and iterative process. It is common to have a totally different set of words at the end of the process. It is all part of the journey.

What do you think your brand is promising to the following groups?

- Participants: _____
- Leader-teachers: _____
- Senior leaders and executives: _____
- Your customers: _____
- Others: _____

Step 5: Identify the differentiators. Consider what differentiates your brand from other learning programs. Is it the people who you serve? The topic or goals of the program? Or something else? Based on those differentiators, adjust the words again to reflect what differentiates this learning program from others.

What makes your brand different from others that are available?

_____

_____

Step 6: Craft a tagline. Finally, craft a few descriptive phrases or taglines. These words help build an understanding of the brand equity—its character, promise, and differentiators—when people are first exposed to it. Create a few different taglines that might be used with different target groups. In the next step, you can test these taglines, along with your logo options, to see which are more appealing to your leader-teachers and future participants. The idea, after all, is to create a personality that attracts them. The brand should be likeable.

What taglines might you use?

_____

_____

_____

Insights from Learning Professionals

Here is how the learning professionals at Radio Flyer related their corporate university brand to the company brand. Radio Flyer is a toy company best known for its popular red toy wagon.

Company Logo

Five words that could be used to characterize our company: fun, kids, memories, smiles, and active.

Wagon University Logo

These same five words characterize Wagon U.

Our tagline is "Grow with us."

To bring our character to life we focus on fun as a part of how we learn. For example, our leaders are teachers who not only bring their energy to the learning program, but also bring engaging tools and Radio Flyer customized curriculum. Fun is injected into the classroom through methods like storytelling, magic tricks, rope games, discussions, and laughter. Fun fuels learning at all ages—whether learning to ride a tricycle or learning advanced communication techniques—we make it a part of our learning environment, and that is how we bring our character to life.

—Radio Flyer material provided courtesy of Amy Bastuga,
Vice President of Human Resources, Radio Flyer

Figure 7.1: Brand Examples

Here are examples of the thinking and results for branding two different multi-program corporate universities.

	R&D University (RDU)	MillerCoors University (MCU)
1. What are you branding?	A training program aimed at increasing innovation in a technical organization	Comprehensive learning solutions that drive the strategic capabilities of the organization
2. What business need is being addressed?	A need for increased cross-fertilization among technologies, brands, and regions to drive innovation	Building the strategic and competitive capability required to win in the market place
3. Who is your target group or audience?	9,000 technical scientists, engineers, and their technical managers at all levels from entry to directors	All 8,500 MillerCoors employees who make, sell, market, and support our portfolio of brands
4. What is your brand character and your brand promise?	• Challenging • Diverse • Global • Strategically connected • Technically advanced	MCU is your business partner that quenches your Thirst for Learning, makes you feel more vital to the enterprise, and helps you achieve business goals.
5. What differentiates this from other brands?	• It's 'For R&D, By R&D,' (R&D leaders teach and are typically two levels above learners) • It's global for maximum networking across all technologies, sciences, and brands to advance innovation opportunities. • It's connected to the R&D strategy and key individual performance factors for ratings and advancement. • It doesn't teach science, because that is handled by CoP training. It is exclusively for the brilliant scientists, engineers, and technical people.	• Leaders teach • Do real work at MCU • Has flexibility and agility • Embedding behaviors • It is about individual capability • It's directly connected to organizational strategy • It's unified with the business and across organizations and functions
6. What are the various taglines?	• For R&D, By R&D • Building Business & Brands by Building Skills & Sharing Knowledge • Today's Learning. Tomorrow's Innovation.	• Real Work • Leaders Teach • Best of You Guide (curriculum guide) • MCU is a progressive enabler of business and personal success
7. What image did you choose?	 Colors: Corporate blue lettering, light blue atom/world, each electron swoop a different color, light blue satellite track	 Colors: golden beer tones in circle (corporate logo) pouring down the graduate cap tassel
8. Where to use the logo and the associated color scheme and brand imagery?	• Invitations to teach and attend • Email correspondence • Website for registration • Website for pre/post-learning • Marketing/deployment materials • All visual elements in classroom (physical and virtual) • Seal of approval: supported by RDU • Thank-you notes	• E-learning templates • Classroom materials • Email messages • Posters and digital signage • Table tents • Videos • Website and LMS • Sell sheets (as for promoting a course or series of courses)

Materials courtesy of Dennis Hirotsu, P&G, Research & Development Manager/VP;
Stephen Buchman, MillerCoors, Director, Learning Operations

Science Notes

Don't shy away from emotional elements of your brand character. Great brands elicit emotions and have been dubbed "Love Marks" (Roberts and Lafley 2005). Brain scientist Donald Calne sums it up: "The essential difference between emotion and reason is that emotion leads to action, while reason leads to conclusions." More emotion, more action.

What Does Your Brand Logo Look Like?

Now comes the fun part—turning your words into an image. Graphic designers are skilled at this. Ask a designer to provide at least three very different images that portray the brand as it is described by the character-words, promise, and tagline. If you don't have access to graphic designers, a do-it-yourself method is available through such online tools as a Google Image search. To get your creative ideas, search on each descriptive word and various combinations of words to see what types of images pop up. Select and combine your favorite images that are consistent with your company and character. (Just be sure you buy the rights to any art or graphics that you plan to use going forward.)

Select images that work well on a big screen and yet are recognizable as a tiny footnote on a PowerPoint, or as part of a signature on an email or letterhead. Consider what your image might look like when done in one color, such as on a coffee mug, pen, or T-shirt.

Now test your logos with your target group. Ask about which images are the best match with the words that describe the character of your brand. Find out which images they like and why. Get a read on their view of the taglines. See Figure 7.2 for an example.

Notice that the final RDU Logo shown in Figure 7.1 is different from all three of those tested in Figure 7.2. The team learned from the research and came up with an alternate graphic that tested well with the target group. It is best to get feedback from those within your target group as early in the process as possible. The feedback will help you get on a desirable path more quickly.

Science Notes

The brain has limited resources, so it welcomes simplification. A logo is a simplification—a mental short cut—that embodies a much larger set of ideas, promises, and experiences.

Figure 7.2: Using Market Research to Create a Strong Brand Image

	Research & Development UNIVERSITY	Research & Development UNIVERSITY	RDU Research & Development UNIVERSITY
1. In your opinion, to what degree does each image represent or match each word below?			
	High Low	High Low	High Low
Challenging	[ ] [ ] [ ] [ ] [ ]	[ ] [ ] [ ] [ ] [ ]	[ ] [ ] [ ] [ ] [ ]
Diverse	[ ] [ ] [ ] [ ] [ ]	[ ] [ ] [ ] [ ] [ ]	[ ] [ ] [ ] [ ] [ ]
Global	[ ] [ ] [ ] [ ] [ ]	[ ] [ ] [ ] [ ] [ ]	[ ] [ ] [ ] [ ] [ ]
Strategically connected	[ ] [ ] [ ] [ ] [ ]	[ ] [ ] [ ] [ ] [ ]	[ ] [ ] [ ] [ ] [ ]
Technically advanced	[ ] [ ] [ ] [ ] [ ]	[ ] [ ] [ ] [ ] [ ]	[ ] [ ] [ ] [ ] [ ]
2. Upon seeing only the images above, which learning program would you prefer to attend? (Choose only one.)			
Please tell us briefly what you prefer about the image you selected.			
3. Which of the three learning programs would you prefer to attend based only on the descriptions provided? (Circle one.)	R&D University For R&D, By R&D	R&D University Building Business & Brands by Building Skills & Sharing Knowledge	R&D University Today's Learning. Tomorrow's Innovation.
Please tell us briefly what you prefer about the description you selected.			

Once your brand logo is designed, tested, revised, and selected, it is time to get the final graphic files and make them available to everyone on the team. It is best to have several different versions of your logo's graphic file because the logo will be used in a wide variety of media. One file should be high resolution so there is no pixilation on a big screen. Another version should be a small file size for use in everyday emails. Be sure to request versions of the file with and without the text or taglines. It would also be smart to get versions with a transparent background, with a white border, a colored border, and a background for use with various background colors that might obscure the image. Graphic artists can help you create templates for screens, slides, and pages that mirror elements in the logo to provide an overall professional look.

How Will You Use Your Brand Logo?

Your brand logo is a mental shortcut. Over time, as more experiences are associated with the brand, a simple glance at the logo will unpack a much larger set of meaning. When you first start using the brand logo, take care to deliver on the promise of the brand. In so doing you are more likely to capture the hearts and minds of your company's best and brightest so that they want to be part of your LAT-related programs and initiatives, all of which will build brand equity as they drive and deliver business results.

To build and maintain awareness, consider where you will use your brand logo and taglines. Look at the list in Figure 7.1 (row 8) for ideas. Build awareness of the brand, and reinforce the brand character and promise every chance you get. Seriously consider who has the right to use your brand. When a program is successful, others may seek to use the brand name. It's happened before that a logo shows up in an unsanctioned, and, often, a lower quality program. On the other hand, the more people who want to be associated with your brand, the better.

Regularly remind your LAT team members of the intended meaning behind your brand. As the program design progresses, ask if choices being made are consistent with the brand character. Use the branding effort to not only define what you are doing, but to be a north star or compass to guide you over time.

Your branding work will dovetail into any internal marketing program you have for the LAT initiative and program launches. Use your brand logo to increase awareness of the programs. As awareness builds, you should hear people mentioning the program in day-to-day conversations, memos, and meetings.

Remind leader-teachers and participants what they can expect from your brand; remind them of the promise behind the brand. You can even ask them directly, "In what ways do you see this program delivering x-y-z [your brand promise]." This type of question builds awareness of your brand equity. As you build brand awareness and a good brand reputation, you are well on your way to making a cultural shift related to who teaches and how they teach. You are set to build momentum for your LAT-culture.

 ## Science Notes

Concrete visual images, like logos, are an excellent way to convey information. The brain appears to have an immediate response to symbols, icons, and other simple images.

 ## Your Turn

Jot down your thoughts on the following topics.

What is it about your brand character that you think will most likely capture the hearts and minds of your company's best and brightest to be part of a leaders-as-teachers program or initiative?

_____

_____

How might you gather evidence about the degree to which the brand and brand reputation that you have, or are creating, is attractive to people? For example, do they want to be part of the program behind the brand?

_____

_____

How might you use your brand logo to build and maintain awareness and gather more LAT supporters and leader-teachers to enable you to continue to drive business results?

_____

_____

Chapter 8

Plan for Change and Build Momentum

"It's easy to make a video about the company's strategy and vision. What is tough is to make sure they are showing it at the plant in Turkey."

—Reuben Mark, former CEO, Colgate Palmolive

■ ■ ■

 Find Your Answers

This chapter focuses on how to grow your LAT approach, integrating it into the culture to assure the benefits continue for years to come. As you read, think about your answers to these questions:

- As you adopt a LAT approach, what is really changing? Who is impacted? What do they give up and what do they gain?
- Which is your next step in John Kotter's classic eight-stage change management process?
- How can the go to the light approach get things started and aid in building momentum?

So far in Part II you have seen tools, stories, models, and more to guide you as you plan for, and design, your own LAT initiative. This chapter guides you to apply classic change management principles to assure that your LAT program can be successfully implemented, and will have lasting impact on your organization.

Learn By Doing:
What Changes and Who Is Impacted

List the roles or people who will be impacted when the LAT approach is implemented, adjusting the list below, as needed, for your organizational setting. For each role, make a list of "what changes" for the people in that role. Take care to check your assumptions. You can gain great insights by talking with a few people about what they think might change. As you gather the "what changes" items, make a note of those things that people might expect to change, but that actually will not change. Lastly, write down what implications these changes might have on the adoption of the LAT approach and acceptance of your organization's LAT-supported initiative.

Who	What Changes	Implication
1. Current trainers		
2. Leader-teachers		
3. Training staff		
4. Leaders not selected as leader-teachers		
5. Learners and participants in learning events		
6.		
7.		
8.		

What Is Changing?

There is a preliminary step to the overall change management process. It is the step of recognizing what changes and what stays the same. When we ask leaders to be teachers, more happens than just changing who stands up in front of a classroom or does the talking on a webinar. The "what" of change will depend on a variety of business and organizational factors and the people with whom you are working. It often helps to think through the "what" in terms of "who." Use the Learn By Doing activity on the previous page to help you think through the process.

Here are some examples of what might change and the implications for the individuals. The workload might increase or decrease, either of which can be desired or can be a concern. Individuals might gain more visibility with people higher or lower in the organizational structure, or with their peers. This might be viewed as risky or a desired opportunity. New skills might need to be developed—again, either an exciting or worrisome prospect, depending on the individual.

Once you have a clearer idea of "what" will change and the implications these changes could have for different people, think through how to adjust your LAT plans to ameliorate negatives, highlight positives, and set up systems for accountability for those aspects that represent needed, yet difficult, changes. With these plans in place, you will be more prepared to lead or be involved in the LAT change management process.

Classic Change Management

The writings of John Kotter on change management have influenced several generations of leaders. Here is a short review of Kotter's eight-stage change process with things to consider relevant to building and growing a LAT approach. As you read through the list, determine the current stage for your LAT team. Use a step-by-step approach as you go through the change process. Experience shows that if a step is missed, forward progress may be hampered until the team returns to that missed step and once again takes up the step-by-step process. A good way to overcome the obstacles to change is to avoid them through careful planning and striving for incremental successes. Going too fast can get in the way. Instead, go slow to move fast.

For more on change management, we recommend the books, *Leading Change* (Kotter 2012) and *The Heart of Change* (Kotter 2012). Additionally, chapter 5 of *Leaders as Teachers* (Betof 2009) delves deeply into this topic.

Quick Tip

Without a sense of urgency, we will do the work when we get around to it.

1. Create a Sense of Urgency

Successful LAT programs revolve around those topics, programs, or activities that have a level of business urgency to them. In the chapter 2 Your Turn you may have already listed key business issues that a LAT approach could help address. While it may feel safer to choose a low risk topic, doing so may not serve the business, nor will it cause cultural and organizational change. Be wary of those who say that nothing will really change. This is an indicator that the plan may be viewed as yet one more flavor of the month. Start with the urgencies that are due to changes in the market, competition, or organizational needs and opportunities.

Learn By Doing: Creating a Sense of Urgency

How do you create a sense of urgency for your LAT initiative? Establish a natural deadline for the project, such as the budget year. Point out the gains when the program is established, such as time savings, reduced errors, speed to market, or reduced costs. Spotlight the risks of not implementing sooner, such as compliance fines, loss of valuable employees, or lack of alignment to the business strategy. List your thoughts here.

_____

_____

_____

_____

_____

_____

2. Establish a Guiding Coalition

A **guiding coalition** usually consists of two or more individuals who drive a successful change initiative. This guiding coalition—often comprised of people on your LAT team—is crucial to the successful adoption of the LAT approach or any change program. Here are two things to watch for. First, assure that the members, together, have enough power to lead the change, and second, that the members work together like a team. Look back to chapter 3, especially Figure 3.4, for more on the elements of effective teams.

Learn By Doing: Who Is Your Guiding Coalition?

List the people who, in your view, are part of your guiding coalition. Now, considering the advice above, do you want to engage anyone else?

_____   _____
_____   _____
_____   _____
_____   _____
_____   _____
_____   _____
_____   _____

3. Create Your Vision and Strategy

A vision is a picture of future success that is painted with words. Find the answers to these questions: What are your goals? What is your scope? How will you succeed? What capabilities are needed to succeed? What management systems are needed? (Lafley, Martin, and Riel 2013). Your notes in the chapter 2 Your Turn section can help you address these questions with clarity and consistency.

Science Notes

Our hunter-gatherer brains view change as a threat. From our brain's perspective, if a bush moves, that is a change, and the brain prepares us for a lion that might be moving behind the bush. But if our brain learns to see a specific type of bush-movement as meaning that there is a bird in the bush for tonight's dinner, the movement and the change is more appealing. Now apply that to today's change. Does your change look more like a threatening lion behind the bush or a tasty bird in the bush?

4. Communicate the Vision

Look at your vision statement and ask yourself if it needs to be restated to be more "our" vision than "my" vision. There is an old African proverb, "If you want to go quickly, go alone. If you want to go far, go together." An organizational vision is most successful in helping to drive change when it is understood and embraced by many. In the end, most of your organization will need to hear it, and they will need to hear it many times in multiple venues and through various media. Only then can it become part of the organization's vocabulary, communications, and most importantly, its culture. Consider two things as you communicate the vision. First, is your guiding coalition role modeling behavior that is consistent with the vision? Second, consider the difference in your state of acceptance and that of others. You and your team have worked long and hard on your vision, goals, and plans, but the people who hear and read about your vision may be hearing it for the first or second time. They are not in the "I'm excited about this, let's move forward" state of mind that you are in. Start with informative communications—facts and goals (Schoemer 2009). As time goes on, and as small LAT successes become greater in number, those receiving your message are likely to adjust to this new idea and can be open to more inspirational communications about the LAT approach.

5. Empower Others for Broad-Based Action

As your LAT culture grows, and more leaders take on the role of **leader-teacher**, keep alert to anything that might become a barrier to continued participation. With the shift in mental models about who teaches and how they teach, there is a need to change support structures to make the new ways easier, rather than to revert to previous methods. For example, when a trainer is needed for a class, is it easier for the course manager to call on a professional trainer because of difficulties in scheduling leader-teachers? Perhaps you can set up one staff member as single point of contact to work with the leader-teachers on scheduling, designating backup leader-teachers as needed. Look toward changing systems to assure that the following are easy to do, rather than obstacles to overcome: preparing materials, scheduling concerns, backup systems, recognition systems, version control, updates for consistency, training tracking management, and training for leader-teachers to help develop their leader-teacher skills. See chapter 11 for a deeper understanding of the needs and ways to address these topics. Lastly, draw more people into LAT programs and have a way to keep track of all those who volunteer or show some interest in becoming a leader-teacher. Call on the people on this list as soon as you are ready to expand your LAT-supported programs.

6. Achieve Short-Term Wins

Plan ahead for visible successes and improvements in performance—these are short-term wins. Frequently, these are precedent-setting events. They are new and different. They begin to change the status quo. The best successes are those that others talk about, the programs that create a "buzz." You can encourage a positive buzz. For example, send thank you notes at the successful completion of a leader-teacher program. The recipient might tell others about the note, or show it to people.

Science Notes

When we give our brains a reason to believe that something is possible, we tend to be more able to duplicate it, in part because our brain is not fighting us by subconsciously repeating "it's not possible!" For example, it was once believed that running a mile in under four minutes was a physical impossibility. Once Roger Bannister did it in 1954, several other runners achieved this same feat within the next year. Let others know what you have accomplished so that they know it is possible and can replicate your feat.

Buzz can be created even before the learning event is scheduled. For example, in savvy and sensitive ways, consider sending a few emails, making a few phone calls, or having a few hallway conversations about any of the following: gaining agreement from a high profile leader to participate in the program, having a great first meeting of the training design team in which leader-teachers participated, or finalizing a great graphic image as part of branding work. Buzz can be created during the event by sharing the news about achieving a high rating from participants for the first half-day of a multi-day leader-teacher supported training program. This softer and less formal messaging often gets a better reception than direct "selling" communication. Use each win to build acceptance and momentum. After establishing the first success, describe the next program as following the successful model of the previous one. A good way for success to become public is through the use of recognition and small rewards for those involved in the early program and teaching successes. This can take the form of a team T-shirt, a recognition lunch, personal thank-you cards, and organization announcements that highlight participants and their successes. A very helpful way to create visible wins is to add a comment about an individual's participation as a leader-teacher in a leader's promotion announcement, performance review, and online profile.

Quick Tip

In the early stages of developing your LAT approach and culture, you create a sense of urgency, establish a guiding coalition, and create and share your vision. Here is a tip to make the next stages actionable as well: Keep a list related to each step so that you can quickly act when the time is right. For example, to empower broad-based action, keep a running list of requests from leader-teachers and others. Use the list during the annual planning season. For the next stage, keep a list of successes to draw upon when it is time to write something for the quarterly newsletter. Gather ideas over time about needed work or systems improvements that would support additional change. Use this list to justify additional staffing, when there is a possibility to bring on an intern or additional staff. Each list used at the right time can advance your LAT culture for the benefit of the business or organization.

7. Consolidate and Build Momentum

Success begets success. Once you have it, use the increased credibility to cause more change in a step-by-step manner. With each new success introduce the next round of changes. It might be the addition of another program, more leader-teachers, or system and policy changes to encourage more of the same while eliminating barriers. This is the time for continuous improvement and appropriate business-based expansion. On a larger scale, next steps might include recruiting and promoting people based on their leader-teacher skills and experience, and developing a pipeline of leader-teachers to meet the various business needs, including the need to develop leaders, in part, by helping them develop their teaching skills both in formal and everyday, in the moment settings.

8. Anchor It in the Culture

You will know that your LAT is part of the culture when you start hearing things like, "that's just how we do it here." However, don't leave this last stage to chance. As Kotter tell us, make a "conscious attempt to show people how specific behaviors and attitudes have helped improve performance. When people are left on their own to make the connections, as is often the case, they can easily create inaccurate links. . . . Anchoring change also requires that sufficient time be taken to ensure that the next generation of management really does personify the new approach. If promotion criteria are not reshaped, another common error, transformations rarely last" (Kotter 2012). Plan now to assure persistent long-term messages about the links between the business and the LAT program. This can help to embed the LAT approach into your culture so that it stays a part of "the way we do it here." The benefits will be worth the effort.

 Insights From Learning Professionals

"At P&G, we have leaders at all levels. There is an army of volunteer employee instructors who deliver core curriculum. When our people teach, we refer to this as 'building the organization' and all managers are truly dedicated to developing others. What surprised me however, when I came into the company as an experienced hire, was that the volunteers also own the courses! If I wanted to change a course, I had to negotiate with the volunteer course owner. This made it hard to establish global standards for quality, or even to assure that materials were up-to-date.

Then I heard how our talent supply (recruiting) structures for governance. With talent supply, volunteers build the organization by recruiting rather than by teaching. These volunteers are organized into what we call school teams. The school team, headed by someone who sits in the business, does the work, but they have final accountability back to the talent supply team. I saw parallels in the processes and asked, 'Can we establish "course teams" like the school teams, which will allow course owners to contribute ideas on content and delivery, but give that final accountability back to Global L&D?'

"We needed governance around our core curriculum, so my approach was to set this up like something that was familiar to P&G, as well as very successful. Managers were all familiar with our school teams, so I introduced course teams with our core curriculum renewal. People bought into the idea very quickly. By repurposing an existing and valued structure, we were able to make a significant improvement to our L&D governance. Now, we have course teams operating successfully in supporting the P&G Leadership Academy, which exemplifies our motto, Excellence in leadership, leaders in learning."

—Ann Schulte, Director, Global Learning & Development, Procter & Gamble

Learn By Doing: Communicate Links Between LAT and Business Needs

How might you begin to communicate to others that LAT is linked to business needs? Would you use this same communication channel for the next few years, or would you add or switch to different communication methods over time? Write down your thoughts about the methods you would use to communicate now and in the future.

_____

_____

_____

Apply the Go to the Light Principle

The **go to the light** principle is about finding the energy within the organization and tapping into it to achieve results. This energy may be centered around individuals, or around a business issue, problem, or opportunity.

Relative to individuals, the go to the light principle taps those people who have the innate energy and interest in the change process you are leading, whether it's a LAT approach or a new strategic organizational initiative. "Most managers try to bring everyone in their organization along with the change by spending 80 percent of their time on 20 percent" of the people who do not agree with the change proposal, says change expert, Karl Schoemer (2009). "Somehow we imagine that if we can turn them, the rest of the change will be easy. That's a major investment of time and emotional energy. All you'll get for your efforts is stress and frustrations." Instead, find those people who embrace your idea with little effort. Go to the people who "get it." More will eventually join in.

Learn By Doing: Identify Your Go to the Light People

List below a few of your own go to the light people—those whom you think will readily engage with the LAT initiative.

_____   _____

_____   _____

_____   _____

At an organizational level, the go to the light principle leverages the energy surrounding organizational issues, business opportunities, and problems. These are likely to have enough energy associated with them to keep the change process moving forward. Change is an energy hog. We refer to change management work as "defying organizational gravity." If a ball is rolled up a hill, gravity will pull it back down. It takes energy to keep that ball moving upward. As you implement change of any kind, keep in mind that "gravity never has a bad day."

In chapter 2 we discussed the importance of implementing the LAT process in a step-by-step manner. It is important to remember that it is highly unlikely that you will be able to quickly create a large-scale LAT change process in the organization. It takes too much energy. In our experience success builds with smaller and successive teaching and program "wins." Link your program to the latest business issues to leverage the energy thrown against those. Nurture those people who are early adopters and who provide the go to the light energy for your change process. Recognize them and reward them with support, helping them succeed in every way that you can.

We encourage you to spend your time and energy as productively as possible. Try the go to the light principle and see if it works for you.

Your Turn

Jot down your thoughts on the following topics

As you think about what is changing and who is impacted, what changes do you think might be the most challenging to manage? How might you begin to address these?

_____

_____

As you read about Kotter's classic eight-stage change process, which three to five ideas did you find most useful? Which of the ideas can you apply next week?

_____

_____

How could the go to the light principle work for your situation? If you apply this principle, how do you see it helping to build momentum for your LAT-supported programs?

_____

_____

Preparing, Delivering, and Evaluating Your LAT Programs

Part III is about helping you execute with excellence for each LAT learning initiative and event that is delivered. There are some differences between delivering a standard learning program and a LAT learning program. These chapters will highlight those differences and provide case studies to help you create a successful LAT program that will yield significant business results.

Chapter 9: Prepare for Success

Preparation is at the heart of excellent execution. Get ready to deliver on the promise of your LAT brand.

Chapter 10: Deliver With Excellence

Learn how to support **leader-teachers** and learners alike in the LAT environment.

Chapter 11: Keep Up the Momentum

Measure, improve, grow, and celebrate successes for your LAT programs. Then get ready to expand your successful programs.

Chapter 12: Build on Your Success

Success begets success, and a successful LAT initiative will generate a demand for more. Learn how to harness that energy through examples from those who have successfully expanded their LAT programs.

Chapter 13: Get Inspired By LAT Success Stories

Read case studies from several Fortune 500 companies to gain insights and encouragement for your own programs.

Chapter 9

Prepare for Success

"Success is to be measured not so much by the position that one has reached in life as by the obstacles which he has overcome while trying to succeed."

—Booker T. Washington

■ ■ ■

 Find Your Answers

As you read about the unique elements of preparing for LAT learning events, think about your answers to these questions:

- What systems can you put in place to help manage unexpected schedule conflicts for leader-teachers?
- What documents and notes will you provide to help leader-teachers succeed?
- What will you do to prepare for a successful LAT-supported learning event?

Learning professionals know how to plan learning events and manage guest speakers. But **leader-teachers** are more than simply guest speakers. They may need different types of support than a professional facilitator. And they might value some different considerations from those offered to subject matter expert trainers. The main differences are in their schedule, leader guide, and preparation.

Schedule

On a macro level, leader-teachers need the day and hour penned into their schedule weeks, months, or even a year in advance. Even then, critical issues can arise that take them from the classroom. It is important to have a backup plan. Common backup plans include using a video taken from a previous session, calling on another leader-teacher who has led this same session in the past, or using team teaching so another leader-teacher is always available.

At the event level, the schedule must clearly specify breaks. It's not unheard of for a first-time leader-teacher to comment, "I didn't know that there were breaks during my four hours of training." Or "so my two hours is really only one hour and forty minutes." Insist that leader-teachers honor break-time. Participants can become disengaged, and even cranky, when they need a break, yet don't want to miss a word that an important leader-teacher has to say. For leader-teachers to be successful, they need to keep participants engaged and willing to apply what is being taught.

For schedules shared with participants, strip out timing, other than the most basic start and stop times, and an indicator of the number of breaks. This gives leader-teachers the flexibility to respond to the participants' energy and interests. This tactic can increase participant engagement, especially if participants are unfamiliar with leader-teacher events and might hesitate to ask a question that could interfere with a break shown on the schedule.

 Quick Tip

For LAT learning events, add five extra minutes to each scheduled break. This lets leader-teachers engage with participants during a break, and reduces timing issues when leader-teachers go beyond their scheduled time. It's a rare LAT event that ends earlier than planned.

Learning From Leader-Teachers

"Helping to create R&D University at P&G was a broadening assignment that was close to my heart. I regularly volunteered to be one of the co-deans for the week. I appreciated the approach of having two deans on hand, especially on one occasion. I recall being in the front of the room in the 'power spot,' as we referred to the trainer's area, when my emergency cell phone rang. Was this a wrong number? I rarely get calls on this phone. I apologized to the class and took the call. I think some of them thought this was part of a learning activity to get their attention on our topic of innovation and change management. It wasn't. But it was a real-life lesson on the topic. As I closed the phone and placed it back in my pocket, I looked out at the more than 50 participants and realized that they could go on without me. 'That was the FDA,' I told the class. 'They are in town for a surprise audit. I have to go. I trust my co-dean to take you through the rest of the day. I hope to see you tomorrow. Mike?' I called to my co-dean, 'You have the class.' With that, I walked out the side door. I was never more thankful for having helped to set up a team-teaching approach for R&D University."

—Dr. Ray Takigiku, CEO Bexion Pharmaceuticals,
formerly Associate Director, P&G Pharmaceuticals

 Insights From Learning Professionals

"Everyone agrees until they see it in writing."

—Jonathan Wilson, Aileron Learning Professional

Leader Guide

When we write things down, we hone our thinking, and we can more easily elicit comments from others. Writing it down also gives us a record for future use for ourselves or for others. Writing is a memory aid. But the level of documentation for each leader-teacher and each learning program can vary greatly. Some use a leader guide that simply lists the start and stop times along with a few bulleted speaking points. Other leader guides are semi-scripted, or even fully scripted.

No matter what level of documentation you use, we have found that leader-teachers typically benefit from a few things: learning objectives, activity instructions, and pre-written discussion questions.

Learning Objectives

Leader-teachers can benefit from an over emphasis on participant-centered learning objectives. Remind them repeatedly that their goal is to confirm that participants can achieve specific learning goals. This encourages leader-teachers to take time to listen to participants and assure that participants understand the material.

Activity Instructions

Help leader-teachers succeed with activities and exercises by providing clear instructions for both the leader-teacher and participants, preferably, in a handout or outlined on the screen. Provide plenty of guidance for leader-teachers on what to do while participants are doing the activity, and how to conduct the all-important debrief. Again, keep the learning objectives front and center for the leader-teacher. See chapter 4 for more on **active teaching**.

Discussion Questions

Great questions engage participants. Bad questions have the opposite effect. Help leader-teachers plan some of their questions in advance. Then provide guidance about how to listen to participants' answers and how to reply—either in class or online. For more, see Skillful Questioning in chapter 4.

Learn By Doing: Documentation Level

Use this list to determine how comprehensive your leader guides should be.

Check all that apply to your situation.

- ☐ Several different leaders will lead the same course at different times or locations.
- ☐ Consistency of message is important across all learning events.
- ☐ The timing is very tight for this learning event.
- ☐ There are more than three topics or leaders (if one runs long, the next must make up the time).
- ☐ There is more than a three month gap between times when the learning event is offered again.
- ☐ The leader is unfamiliar with the topic.
- ☐ The leader-teachers might benefit from teaching tips that are embedded into the materials.

Minimal: If no items apply, you might choose to use a minimalistic approach: start and stop time, a few key bullet points on the topic, and the participant goals or learning objectives.

Semi-Scripted: If a few items are checked, consider a semi-scripted approach that includes cues such as "add a personal and relevant story here" and "ask this question to drive discussion."

Heavily Scripted: If most or all items are checked, a heavily scripted leader guide might serve you well, complete with a checklist of points to cover for each visual, notes as to when to tell personal stories, a list of questions to ask to drive discussion, tips on when to click the mouse to build the slide, a set of frequently asked questions with appropriate responses, call outs for activities so these go as planned, and supplemental reading to build the leader-teacher's topical knowledge.

Preparation

Preparation is at the heart of excellent execution; it is the process of visualizing the future to assure that everything is in place for success. With leader-teachers, three elements warrant particular attention: logistical details, trainer training and practice, and preparing the leader-teachers and participants to interact.

Logistical Details

The last thing a leader-teacher has time to worry about is the logistical details. Have a plan for taking care of the details, such as reserving a room, setting up a webinar, printing handouts, enrolling the right number of participants, and confirming compatibility of the software and hardware. A mistake here can spiral into a big negative for your LAT program. Plan to get it right.

Version control can become a headache with leader-teachers if they are accustomed to preparing their business presentations and making numerous last minute changes. Make sure there are robust systems in place for managing such things as leader-teacher additions and changes to handouts, slides, or extra video clips they bring, which pose potential audio compatibility issues.

Be ready for enthusiastic leader-teachers. It can help if you build a strong rapport with your leader-teachers and encourage them to tell you quickly about any last minute change of plans. In their enthusiasm, they may not be thinking of the logistical consequences of their desire to provide participants with the most up-to-date information, or to share the class with others by inviting them to attend the class as an observer or participant. Be ready to accommodate their enthusiasm as much as possible. Enthusiasm is a good thing.

 Learning From Leader-Teachers

"The practice of leaders as teachers in our leadership development programs made a lasting impact on me as a leader. The preparation for teaching was intense and required me to study and become somewhat of a subject matter expert on the relevant topics. This was necessary to truly be viewed as a teacher, and preparing real world examples to supplement the topic made the learning even more impactful. The students learned a lot more by sharing the mistakes and successes we as leaders had made during our careers. I became a better leader through the debate, challenge, and exploration of many topics that we covered in our programs."

—Jay Glasscock, Vice President/General Manager, Thermo Fisher

Learning From Leader-Teachers

When asked what the learning department can do to best support leader-teachers, John Leikhim retired manager/VP of research and development at P&G said, "I think the training experts can make it easy. The training experts can take the leader's subject matter and their expertise, and shape it into material that the leader can deliver with confidence. Not everybody is a training expert, so having training experts shape it in a way that people can learn from is important. Particularly with today's generation, and people learning from different media—the training experts help shape it so others can learn from it." Leikhim says he counted on the staff to "make sure everything is ready. You need to take the mundane and time-consuming details away from the people (leader-teachers) so they don't have to worry. You can make it easy."

Trainer Training and Practice

Providing opportunities to practice and conduct dry runs is crucial for leader-teachers for several reasons. First, leader-teachers typically do not have formal training in facilitation. Second, they don't have much time to practice, unless you help them by putting practice time on their calendars. Third, leader-teachers need feedback on how they are doing as teachers.

For online learning events, as much as possible, have a technical "co-pilot" work with the leader-teachers. Do dry runs to help the pair gain experience working together as a team. For example, if a question is sent in using chat, how would the leader-teacher like to be alerted? Individual leader-teachers must learn, through experience, which method—a note slipped to them, a tug at the sleeve and pointing, a text message—will allow them to respond without totally losing their train of thought.

While it would be ideal to insist that leader-teachers take formal trainer training, more often, their schedules dictate private or small-group practice and trainer-training sessions. See the Banner Health and SES case studies in chapter 12 for more about both methods. During practice, be sure to tell leader-teachers what they are doing right to build their confidence and help them improve. Provide them with alternate options for those things they are not doing well. Focus on platform skills that improve interaction with participants, as opposed to a lecture or presentation style. Help them judge their timing and prepare them to leave twice as much time as they expect for interaction with participants.

Focus their practice time on the first, last, and interactive parts of the learning event. The first part is when the leader-teacher is getting mentally in sync with the participants. It's when nervousness can interfere. Practicing the beginning moments is a good way to get off to a great start. Likewise, practice the last section and close of the learning event. Again, nerves can be high at this point as the final minutes tick away and there is still so much more to discuss. Plan suitable ways to wrap it up, whether the program is on-time, overtime, or ahead of time. Regardless, the time spent practicing will pay off in the end.

Preparing the Leader-Teachers and Participants to Interact

The learning event will be more successful if the leader-teachers and participants are both prepared to interact. This is a two-way street that is best paved ahead of time. Things you can do to pave the way include introducing leader-teachers to participants in advance of the learning event, acquainting leader-teachers with the level of sophistication and knowledge participants have on this topic, and setting expectations with participants in advance of the learning event.

Introducing Leader-Teachers and Participants

These introductions before the event can be as simple as providing participants with a bio of the leader-teachers and providing leader-teachers with a class list. This eliminates some surprises. Don't let participants learn at the last minute that their boss is teaching! Likewise, give leader-teachers a chance to identify participants who are known entities. By providing a bio of the leader-teacher in advance, it can save very valuable face-to-face time that might be spent covering the leader-teacher's accomplishments at the start of a learning event.

Share Participants' Knowledge of the Topic

This knowledge can be gathered through the use of pre-work. In pre-work, ask questions about the topic or about something you've asked them to read before class begins. The level of sophistication of the participants' responses will inform the leader-teacher about the level of knowledge and familiarity, or misconceptions, on the topic. Additionally, if there is significant variation among the participants' knowledge, plans can be put in place to manage this. Knowing the participants' level of knowledge helps leader-teachers successfully communicate at the level needed for each group. Further, pre-work can be used to reinforce the expectation that participants and leader-teachers will actively interact during the session. Lastly, with the pre-work in hand, a leader-teacher can quickly engage participants by turning the spotlight on the participants with an initial comment such as, "I was reading your pre-work over the last few days, and I observed that. . . ." With this simple comment, participants know that the leader-teacher cares enough to prepare and read their comments. That's a great way to kick off a learning event.

Set Expectations

Setting expectations for participants about pre-work, post-work, and engagement during the learning event, will help them more fully engage with leader-teachers and help assure that the result of the learning event will be noticeable in the workplace. After all, the purpose of having leaders-as-teachers is to make an impact on the business. Consider the following as possible expectations that you might set for participants.

 Quick Tip

If there are no implications for skipping the pre-learning, few of your busy learners will do it. Yet you know that the pre-work is carefully selected to help them interact during the learning event and learn at a deeper level. So, add a consequence. A common one goes something like this: "All of your pre-learning responses must be online five days prior to the start of the session. This is when our leader-teachers will have access to all of your answers and will begin reviewing your responses in preparation for the learning event."

Learn By Doing: Setting Expectations

Which expectations might you need to set? Check off items from the list below and add a few more that apply to your situation. Then consider how you will communicate the expectation: As part of a registration message? Within the description of the program? Contained within instructions for attending or for completing pre-work? As part of a welcome message at the learning event itself?

Needed?	Learning Expectations	How and When to Set It
☐	**Come prepared to engage!** This is an active learning experience, not a passive lecture-based class. (If people are not accustomed to interacting with leader-teachers, consider addressing this.)	
☐	**Explain your learning experience time-period.** Cover total duration (days, weeks, months) and an estimate of time engaged in learning, pre-work, pre-learning, the learning event, evening activities, and post-learning activities.	
☐	**Type of pre-work and pre-learning.** What is it? How much time will it take? Who sees responses? Who can help with questions? What are the consequences of incomplete work? What is the value of this expenditure of time and energy?	
☐	**Learning is hard work!** Include a description of the expected environment—challenging, collaborative, competitive, insightful, or thought-provoking. Assure that everyone knows this is not a day off from work; it is work.	
☐	**Type of post-learning.** What is it? How much time will it take? Who sees responses? Who and what resources are available? What are the consequences of incomplete work? What is the value of this expenditure of time and energy?	
☐	**Other learning expectations:**	

Learning From Leader-Teachers

"Our researchers and scientists inevitably questioned why they must complete five hours of pre-work before attending a four-day training program. Eventually, the staff created a 'Why So Much Pre-Work' message and sent it out, automatically, three weeks prior to the event. Here's one version of it.

Some of you have asked why there is so much pre-learning assigned before R&D Colleges. Pre-work (1) prepares the brain to learn, (2) assures that everyone has mastered the same language and concepts prior to group activities, and (3) is used to form teams for specific exercises. For entry-level programs you are asked to do five hours of pre-work and this increases to more than 20 hours for higher level programs.

While you may not see or hear a direct reference to each pre-work item during the program, each item has a specific purpose and use. We do our best not to repeat in class what you covered in pre-work, but we do build on it. We expect you to master the pre-work material and use the in-person lessons during the college itself to take the material to the next level'

"This message went a long way to helping participants both understand the reason for the effort and prioritize the pre-learning work."

—Ken Edelman, Leader-Teacher for R&D University, P&G

Your Turn

Jot down your thoughts on the following topics.

For your LAT programs, what type of documentation do you think will meet the needs of most leader-teachers in your organization?

_____

_____

How might you help leader-teachers prepare to teach? What will build their confidence and teaching-expertise to assure effective learning for participants?

_____

_____

What preparations have you read about in this chapter that will help in your situation? Which idea will you implement first? Which ideas would you like to implement in the future?

_____

_____

Considering your workplace culture relative to planning, how might this culture help or hinder the goal of being prepared to deliver an excellent LAT-enabled learning event? What might you do to tap into or mitigate the cultural aspects relative to planning?

_____

_____

Chapter 10

Deliver With Excellence

"Organizations don't execute unless the right people, individually and collectively, focus on the right details at the right time."

—Larry Bossidy and Ram Charan

■ ■ ■

 Find Your Answers

It is showtime, and this is not the time to let leader-teachers go solo. Instead, this chapter gives you a glimpse at what can be done to support leader-teachers at the moment they engage with participants. As you read, think about your answers to these questions.

- What support will benefit leader-teachers during the learning event?
- How can you support leader-teachers when they interact with participants through either your advanced preparations or your own in the moment actions?
- What actions can you take after leader-teachers complete the learning event in order to ensure continued excellence the next time?

Effective teaching requires preparations over the weeks and months before the training program. Now, as the **leader-teachers** begin to engage with participants, there are three types of support that most leader-teachers value: general support, a professional trainer's advice, and assistance to ensure continued excellence for next time.

General Support

Professional facilitators and experienced trainers manage many things in the classroom. Think through these normal things and try to determine if they are things a learning professional or staff member should help the leader-teacher with, or not. Consider, for example, these three areas: nervousness, logistics, and participant management. While leader-teachers are likely skilled at managing each of these on the job, they may be managed differently in the classroom. As described in this section, it can make a big difference for leader-teachers to get support from staff and learning professionals in these areas.

Combat Nervous Tension

We all know that speaking in front of a group of people can be a nerve-racking experience. Leaders at all levels feel it. When teaching, some leaders may feel it more than usual. Successful LAT programs address this natural discomfort. The key is to create a leader-teacher experience that is as stress-free and enjoyable as possible to keep them coming back for more. This applies to web-based training and live virtual learning events, just as much as it does to common classroom experiences.

Use the tips in the Learn By Doing activity to assist leader-teachers through their nervousness. Most will become less nervous either as the learning event proceeds or as they participate in more learning events. For some, an external coach can help. Remind them that participants are truly interested in what they have to say. For the most part, participants sympathize with a speaker who is nervous, and they want their leader-teachers to be successful, not only in business, but also in the classroom.

Learn By Doing:
Combat Nervous Tension

Check the items that you think your leader-teachers might value to help them combat nervous tension. As much as possible, build a relationship with each leader-teacher to help you understand which elements will likely help each person.

☐ Make sure leader-teachers can arrive 30 to 60 minutes early to become comfortable, do final preparation, and interact with participants as they arrive.

☐ Encourage leader-teachers to step into the physical space beforehand to gain familiarity.

☐ Provide last minute calming words. (You need to establish a relationship with each leader-teacher to know what will be calming for them, and what other support you can offer to help them feel comfortable and confident.)

☐ Encourage leader-teachers to focus on the learners instead of themselves to reduce nerves.

☐ Confirm a method the leader-teacher will use as their first activity to engage participants within 30 seconds at the start of the session. This is referred to as turning the spotlight on the participants.

☐ Offer water before and during the session to combat dry mouth. Keep the water close at hand to avoid awkward moments of reaching for, or trying to find the water.

☐ Your ideas: _____

_____

_____

 # Science Notes

Breathe deep! When we breathe deep, we activate the vagus nerve that triggers the release of acetylcholine. This neurotransmitter is responsible not only for calming and relaxation, but also for learning and memory. Encourage your learners and leader-teachers to breathe deep!

Handle Onsite Logistics

The last thing a leader-teacher needs to do is to figure out where the handouts are, how to get the projector hooked up, how to use the mouse-advancer, or how to get the video to play on the screen at the right volume level. Take care of these things for leaders so that they can focus on interacting with participants.

Learn By Doing:
Handle Logistics

Check each item that needs to be handled in your situation. Make a plan for each checked item.

- ☐ A way to manage handouts.
- ☐ Arrange for someone to handle audio/video elements. Let leader-teachers know they are there to share wisdom, not demonstrate audio/visual prowess.
- ☐ Provide ready access to participant materials so that the leader-teacher knows what the participants are seeing.
- ☐ Arrange to keep external distractions to a minimum—noise, people coming in and out, and so on.
- ☐ Your ideas: _____
  _____
  _____

Science Notes

The brain values certainty. When complexity surrounds us, it helps to be able to focus on one thing with certainty. A checklist that reflects the wisdom of the team's thinking and planning, can provide the certainty we crave when under pressure to deliver an excellent learning event.

Manage Participants

While the leader-teachers engage with the group of participants on the subject matter, they often appreciate a helping hand with the one or two participants who need special attention. To address the late-comers, the people who get sick, those who can't find their handouts, or those who can't log-on to the website, agree in advance with the leader-teacher that someone on your support team will work with these people to minimize distractions. This agreement can help to avoid potential embarrassment for the participant too.

A particularly sensitive issue to manage is people who leave the training. If a few learners step out (virtually or in live classes) for long periods of time, this can negatively impact other learners who may think: "what happened to the person?" "can I leave too?," "how embarrassing for the leader-teacher," or "it's not fair that my team is missing a member." Staff and leader-teachers should, at some level, indicate their awareness of the situation to put learners at ease. You can help leader-teachers by discussing, in advance, situations such as those shown on the following page.

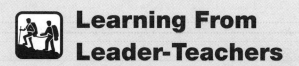

Learning From Leader-Teachers

"My role as a leader-teacher has provided me with insights into the organization that I likely would not have gotten in other ways. Specifically, the classroom dynamic that positions me as a teacher, not an executive, has encouraged the participants to speak more freely than they would in other settings. The classroom is a safe environment where participants are able to ask challenging questions, and since we use real examples from around the company, participants are able to challenge company strategy and performance in a very safe way. From their questions and the resulting discussion I have been able to identify many opportunities for us to improve and strengthen the strategy, as well as to optimize the implementation plans. It is very much a win-win for myself and the participants."

—Stephen Sichak, Senior Vice President, Integrated Supply Chain, BD

Learn By Doing:
Dealing With Absent Participants

Look at the suggestions below for ways to manage people who leave the class. Note when it might be right for you and your leader-teachers to use these ideas.

☐ The event leader establishes ground rules early on, related to showing respect for each other, especially regarding taking phone calls and sticking with the class.

_____

_____

☐ A leader-teacher notes several learners leaving and suggests a bio-break (bathroom, refresh beverages, and stand and stretch).

_____

_____

☐ Leader-teachers can acknowledge that someone has suddenly and inexplicable left the class by commenting, when appropriate, that they noticed Chris left, and ask for a volunteer to bring Chris up to speed if and when he returns.

_____

_____

☐ Staff seeks out missing participants to offer assistance, encourage them to prioritize the learning, or consider signing up for the next class due to other priorities.

_____

_____

Professional Advice

Even for skilled trainers, there can be a lot going on during a learning event. When possible, consider providing leader-teachers assistance with increasing participant interaction, reinforcing good facilitation skills with tips and feedback, and providing help to get back on schedule.

Increasing Participant Interaction

Leader-teachers can benefit from an L&D professional's help with a quiet or passive class. When learners are interacting with leader-teachers, a natural stress can develop based on a desire to look good and not to be embarrassed. This is particularly apparent when a leader-teacher asks a group of learners a question. Some people will not respond aloud, others will be the first to respond almost every time, and others will contribute after someone else has given a first response to break the ice.

Part of the reason for this difference is people's natural comfort levels in groups. Another part of this difference relates to the variation in people's response formulation times—time to simply process the question, additional time to formulate a response, and even more time to get up enough courage to speak out. Leveling out the response times can help more learners become engaged in the process of learning.

Learn By Doing: Getting More People to Interact With Leader-Teachers

Here are some methods that can help get all participants involved. You might share these with leader-teachers as part of helping them prepare to teach, or you might suggest one or more of these methods during the learning event, based on your sense of how the learner group is responding to the leader-teacher. For each method, note which ones you have seen or used, and which you would like to try at the next opportunity.

Method	The leader-teacher says:	Seen? Use? Try?
Chart pad responses	"On a sticky note, write down one possible solution to this question. Then post your answers on the chart pad with a heading that best categorizes your idea." (Example: When brainstorming ways to simplify a work process, chart pads might have headings such as System, Work Process, Decision Making, Equipment, or IT program)	
Individual, small group, large group	"Jot down your thoughts on this question. After xx time (30 sec to two min), share your thoughts with one or two people in your group." After a few more minutes, say, "I'd like to ask that the small groups share a strong thought with your larger group, and in a few minutes, let's have a spokesperson for each group share just one thought from your group with all of us."	
Response by group	After one person has responded to the leader-teacher's question, ask "What about someone from a different group?" the leader-teacher might call on several groups. Do this a few times and it will begin to happen more naturally.	
Wait a moment	"Let me ask you a question. Think about it for a moment. Then I'd like to hear a few responses."	

Reinforce Good Facilitation Skills

As you develop a rapport with leader-teachers during the preparation stages, you will likely note the skills each person is intentionally trying to build. As they conduct the learning event, make a point of observing how they are doing in these areas. At an appropriate time, give them feedback to let them know what improvements you are seeing. For example, a leader-teacher might be working on her ability to ask better discussion questions, learning how to more fluidly move around the room to interact with participants, or how to smoothly integrate responses to online chat questions into the dialog. Others might ask for you to assist them with pre-arranged signals when they fall back into an undesirable habit, like talking too fast or using words and phrases that do not translate well for people whose primary language is different. More examples are listed in the Learn By Doing activity below.

 # Learn By Doing:
Facilitation Help and Tips

Check the items your leader-teachers might appreciate help on during a learning event.

- ☐ Have a large clock readily available and a plan to alert them to the time during the session.
- ☐ Design a way to remind leader-teachers if you see them falling back into a distracting behavior, such as pacing or pen clicking.
- ☐ Use a pre-arranged signal if dialog is going on too long or is off-track.
- ☐ Set the expectation that some topics will be posted on a "parking lot" to be addressed later.
- ☐ Your ideas: _____

_____

_____

Provide Help to Get Back on Schedule

L&D professionals regularly face the dilemma of taking time to meet the apparent needs and interests of the participant group versus the desire to complete all of the program's learning objectives. When leader-teachers face these situations, it helps to have a neutral party talk to them about how to get back on track. You might share the template on the following page with leader-teachers to help them further develop their teaching skills.

Learn By Doing: Getting Back on Schedule

Read the items to consider when to make decisions about timing versus content. Then look at what might be done to get back on track. Now, think about a time when you faced a serious schedule-versus-content dilemma. Check off the considerations that applied and select the options, or combination of options, you might use should this situation arise again.

Considerations

Is the content critical, such as...

- ☐ part of compliance training and required by law
- ☐ part of a certification program that requires core content
- ☐ a pre-requisite for the next part of the program?

Is the extra time-on-topic due to...

- ☐ a small percentage of the class who needs additional help to master the content
- ☐ a response to high interest by most participants
- ☐ the leader-teacher's high interest on the subject
- ☐ the leader-teacher's desire to learn more about how participants view this topic?

Options for getting back on track

Shift the content—preferably the non-crucial content—outside the boundaries of the class by...

- ☐ providing written material for reading later
- ☐ offering a discussion during break or after the learning event
- ☐ placing the topic on a "parking lot" for later discussion
- ☐ agreeing to follow up on the topic by phone or an additional conference call in the future.

Trim time in other areas, using such methods as:

- ☐ reducing break and meal times slightly (Caution: These are important for networking and processing learning.)
- ☐ reducing time on small-group report-outs by
    - ■ having only two groups report out and others list on a chart pad the elements in their report not covered in the oral responses.
    - ■ decrease the number of small groups by increasing the number of people in each team by one or two people.
- ☐ convert an interactive discussion to a mini-lecture. (Caution: Learning recall will be lower on this element, so chose the topic appropriately.)

Having to cut back on content or interaction for a learning event is never a good situation, but it happens regularly. After the learning event, try to determine if this was a one-time event or if the learning program could benefit from a redesign to either extend the learning event time or reduce the content of the program.

Whether it's a schedule-versus-content dilemma, or another classroom management issue, leader-teachers can benefit from the advice of a learning professional, as you can see from the next Insights From Learning Professionals story.

 Insights From Learning Professionals

"The tone you set at the launch of your LAT program makes a difference. The CEO and his executive team chartered and staffed a program to develop leadership capability for leaders with high executive potential. Three weeks before the program, participants received a packet of pre-work including articles, inventories, and worksheets. The importance of completing the pre-work before arriving at the program was made very clear. Early on the first day of the week-long program, it became evident that four of the participants did not complete the pre-work. This was an impediment to their learning as well as the learning of the other participants. When it came time to form small breakout groups, the four were put together. When it came time for the small groups to report-out on their activity, despite their best efforts, the foursome clearly was not contributing at the level of the other groups.

"Call it peer pressure, embarrassment, guilt, or whatever, but the following day, it was clear that they were up late the night before and highly prepared for day two of the program and subsequently prepared every day for the rest of the week. Weeks later, we heard that the word got out to future participants: under no circumstances, should anyone arrive unprepared for this program. No participant ever arrived again without completing the six to eight hours of pre-work. A coincidence? We don't think so. This first group set the tone and created the buzz for the next four years that this program was offered. This expectation that you must be prepared even extended into the post-program action plans. Subsequently, many of the initial participants became leader-teachers in this same program. They modeled the expectation that it was essential to be prepared and, as a result, everyone benefitted and learned."

—Learning leader of a global healthcare company

Quick Tip

Team teaching is a good **silo-busting** tactic when teams are made up of leader-teachers from different parts of the organization. Time spent together at a learning event is a key part of the silo-busting process as leader-teachers greet one another and catch up on work and life in general.

Ensure Continued Excellence

As each leader-teacher completes their part of the learning program, it is time for the LAT champions to think about success for the next time! Consider what you can do immediately, before leader-teachers leave the area, and shortly after the event, to ensure that leader-teachers feel fulfilled in their roles and committed to continuing to lead by teaching.

Immediately

When a learning segment is complete, and the schedule calls for a break, the leader-teacher often will be surrounded by participants with additional questions and comments. Encourage leaders to move these impromptu Q&A sessions out to the break area so that the room can be set up for the next session. This shift to a place outside the classroom also encourages more mingling with participants in a less formal setting.

If possible, encourage leader-teachers to stay for the next break, meal, or session. Encourage them to interact with participants as well as with other leader-teachers. This post-session interaction time is ideal for interaction among people from different parts of the organization.

Before They Leave

Before leader-teachers leave, be sure to check their satisfaction with the experience. A simple question like, "How do you think it went?" becomes a great source of feedback, as well as a way to help the leader-teacher debrief and cool down after a stimulating session. Depending on the personality of the leader-teacher and the nature of the topic and participant group, you will likely hear such things as, "Great! When is the next one?" or "Wonderful, and could you make sure that the one slide I mentioned is updated for me for next time?" to "This was a tough one. We need to rework that one activity to allow more time." or "Great. This group was terrific! I'm counting on you to get those extra parking lot questions to me so I can answer them."

It is important to give leader-teachers this moment to reflect on what has just happened during this teaching segment. In addition, it is good practice to debrief with faculty—both staff and leader-teachers—to identify what went well and what needs adjusting.

Shortly After the Event

Commitments will have been made during the learning event, often by leader-teachers. Meeting every commitment builds a strong reputation for your LAT approach. It is a good idea to assign a staff member to help keep track of both the commitments and the follow through. Your leader-teachers should have full confidence that the staff will help with reminders so that their personal reputation for follow through is upheld. Further, if you handle it right, these items can also serve as a reminder of the LAT program, just as regular advertising reminds consumers to keep buying the brand. On the following page is a list of common commitment items and some tips on how to use them to keep leader-teachers involved.

By following up in a timely manner, and by being thorough in meeting all commitments, you enhance the reputation of the LAT program and build brand equity. Here is an example. A leader-teacher notices that a statistic used in the presentation material is out of date and asks a staff member to fix it before the next class. The LAT program gains credibility as being "easy for leader-teachers to do" when the number is corrected and the correct version of the material is used at the next class. Participants will generate a positive buzz when everyone gets the promised emails, links, and materials.

When the learning event is delivered with excellence, and when leader-teachers feel that they have been successful during the event, your LAT program is bound to succeed, and likely to expand.

Learn By Doing:
Follow Up on Commitments

As you read the common items that require follow-up, check off those that you are likely to encounter. Think about who will do these, and how it might get done. Also note the ways that these items might be used to keep the LAT programs front-of-mind for leader-teachers.

Follow-Up Item	Keep Leader-Teachers in Mind
☐ Type up flip charts or other materials created in class and share with participants and faculty.	• CC leader-teacher.
☐ Collect photos from the participants (typically from smartphones) to post and share.	• CC leader-teacher on link, maybe sharing a favorite photo of them.
☐ Gather online chat messages, clean them up, and post/share.	• CC leader-teacher or ask them to send to distribution list.
☐ Send participants links to training materials used during the session.	• CC leader-teachers.
☐ Share class/cohort list with contact information to participants and/or faculty.	• CC leader-teachers.
☐ Post training materials for participants' use.	• CC leader-teachers or ask them to send.
☐ Send request to participants' managers to discuss program-related action plans.	• CC leader-teachers or ask them to send (provide the distribution list).
☐ Send files or links to material that a leader-teacher said would be shared.	• CC leader-teachers or remind them to send, and provide the distribution list.
☐ Send a message to faculty about participant evaluation ratings of the learning event.	• CC leader-teachers with a thank you for their contributions to good ratings.
☐ Collect all potentially confidential materials and manage these appropriately.	• Confirm disposal of confidential materials used by the leader-teacher.
☐ Make program revisions, changes, and updates as discussed during post-session debrief.	• Confirm that changes requested by the leader-teacher have been completed.
☐ Follow up on any remaining "parking lot" list items from the program.	• Confirm with leader-teacher that these are done or enlist their assistance.
☐ Return any items that were left behind.	• Even leader-teachers leave items behind.
☐ Send post-session assignments.	• Get leader-teacher quote on the importance of completing these assignments.
☐ Send certificates of completion or attendance.	• Leader-teacher might sign these.
☐ Other: _____	
☐ Other: _____	

Your Turn

Jot down your thoughts on the following topics.

How will you go about discovering what type of support would be most helpful for each of your leader-teachers?

_____

_____

After reading this chapter, are there any new things you would like to do to provide support for leader-teachers as they engage with participants?

_____

_____

As the learning event concludes, what would you like to do to help leader-teachers succeed again and again?

_____

_____

In your workplace culture, what are the current practices for supporting learning event leaders, trainers, facilitators, and teachers? As more leader-teachers join the faculty, will you re-apply current practices and/or introduce different practices in order to positively impact the learning events and, ultimately, the business results?

_____

_____

Chapter 11

Keep Up the Momentum

"We now accept the fact that learning is a lifelong process of keeping abreast of change. And the most pressing task is to teach people how to learn."

—Peter Drucker

■ ■ ■

 Find Your Answers

When the learning event is over, it's not really over. As you read this, consider these questions:

- What is an appropriate celebration for leader-teachers and partici-pants after a learning event?
- How can leader-teachers support participants as they start to apply what was learned?
- How might you define "success" for LAT events, and how can you use this success to bolster the positive reputation of your LAT brand?

Leader-teachers and participants alike will have put tremendous energy into teaching and learning for LAT learning events. Now it's up to you to keep the momentum going. There are three areas that can help in this regard. First, cele-brate successes and recognize those who contributed to the success. Next, follow up on the application of learning in the workplace. After all, we want to assure that all this energy is having a positive impact on the business. Lastly, do a quick check on your LAT team to confirm team effectiveness.

Celebrate Success

As the learning event wraps up, there are so many successes to celebrate and contributors to recognize. Below is a list of possible ways to celebrate. These celebrations are important to mark successful completion of one phase of the learning program before moving to the next phase; to provide space for thanks, appreciation, and admiration among faculty, staff, and participants; and to give time for those involved to reflect on what they have accomplished. This process of celebration tends to build positive energy for all involved.

 # Learn By Doing: Celebrate

Celebrations can be formal and informal. The celebration can be for leader-teachers (LT), faculty (F), staff present at the event (S), participants (P), and behind-the-scenes contributors (C). For each celebration description, check off which of the groups might appreciate this approach.

Celebrate Success	LT	F	S	P	C
Plan a ceremony to award certificates of completion, with high energy, lots of applause, and maybe a chance to shake hands with key leader-teachers.					
Plan a celebratory lunch or dinner immediately after the event.					
Send a desk or wall item (such as a plaque) with the learning program logo, and possibly with participants' names engraved.					
Write personal thank-you notes.					
Send a general thank-you note with a few highlights about the success.					
Capture key knowledge artistically and present several categories of awards.					
Make follow-up calls to offer verbal thanks and appreciation.					
Give a small gift such as a cutting-edge book or gift card.					
Provide a polo or T-shirt with the learning event or organization logo.					
Include a thank-you note in the next quarterly organization newsletter.					
On a website or company news page, post a thank-you note and list all who contributed to the program's success.					
Do an "appreciation" activity, during the program or a team meeting, in which everyone writes something they appreciate about everyone else on a small sticky note. Each person walks out with several of these notes.					
Send notes of acknowledgement to the individuals' managers.					
Other: _____					

Follow Up on Learning Application and Business Impact

Much of a leader-teacher's satisfaction comes in having had an important role in the development of associates and leaders, as well as in participants' successful application of learning, which can strengthen individual, team, and organizational performance. This next section focuses on how you can drive application after learning events, collect success stories about learning that has been applied, and present the LAT-related successes with a scorecard or report.

Drive Application

Every leader-teacher's success is predicated on the assumption that the participants will learn and apply what they learn. The LAT initiative team can help to turn that assumption into a reality by supporting post-learning event application.

After a learning event, the neural pathways related to the learning can be strengthened with reminders. A simple approach is to send reminders at three days, three weeks, and three months after the event. It might be as simple as sending an email after three days with the program logo and name of the learning event. At three weeks, you might send the class photo. Sure, you could send it earlier, but hold off and use this "memory candy" for the three-week reminder. At three months, a good choice is to return a copy or a website link to the learners' own written commitments to apply the learning. With these reminders, ask participants to reply with a story about one thing they applied from the learning event that they most appreciate now.

Better yet, get leader-teachers involved, asking them to send prepared messages to participants, and watch replies come in. (See more on collecting stories below.)

The best method to help learners apply learning in the workplace is to assign and track a post-learning activity. A post-learning activity is something that is agreed upon before or during the learning event. Participants could self-select the project, or be assigned to work with a team. Because day-to-day work can pull participants back into their normal routine, it is important to help them track the progress of their post-learning activities. Leader-teachers can help motivate participants to complete these activities by showing a personal interest, either with a simple email or phone call, or by taking a more dynamic role, such as agreeing to act as coaches, mentors, or reviewers of the completed projects.

The most common post-learning activities include personal commitment lists, follow-up agreements with the learners' managers, prearranged coaching sessions for several months following the program, teach-back commitments, and team support for application over the next four to 12 months.

One of the strongest methods to ensure learning transfer is post-event activities. These remind participants that learning programs can only impact business performance if they apply what they learn. As much as possible, engage leader-teachers in this element of the learning program, too, to provide additional opportunities to **teach in the moment** (see chapter 5). In these immediate teaching and coaching moments, leaders are more likely to hear, first hand, the success stories resulting from their teaching efforts.

Collect Stories

With each learning program, participants will have stories of success they experienced as a direct result of what they learned from their leader-teachers. This anecdotal evidence bolsters credibility and goes a long way to illustrate to senior leaders that the program is making a difference. One very powerful method of demonstrating the value of LAT-supported learning events is to share a collection of these examples and stories.

Help your leader-teachers collect stories about participant successes. These stories will be repeated in executive leadership meetings, in casual conversations, and even outside the workplace by leader-teachers who are rightfully pleased to have had a positive impact on others. Having worked hard at teaching, leader-teachers are rewarded intrinsically when they hear stories about the impact of their work.

Now think about how you will share these stories with other leader-teachers to bolster the reputation of LAT as a program that contributes to achieving business goals. Some of these stories can be personal so use care and your political wisdom as you share. While some stories might be best shared quietly and privately with the leader-teachers involved or with your leader-teacher teams, others can be printed in the company newsletter or quoted as part of an awareness-building effort when recruiting the next class's participants or leader-teachers. Either way, collect, share, and tell stories about participant successes to build the reputation your LAT.

Learn By Doing: Collecting Stories

Here are two true stories that reflect the value of various leader-teacher led learning events. As you read these, note how the story came to be known, and consider how you could tap this methodology to collect stories where you work.

Story 1: The leader-teacher taught a coaching technique that required asking questions to guide an employee to his own answers, and not telling the employee "the" answer. The next day, one participant asked the leader-teacher if he could address the class about his experience with this method. The participant reported that one of his key employees called, during training the previous day, to turn in his notice of resignation. This was completely unexpected. The participant and his direct report agreed to meet for dinner to talk. At dinner, the employee shared that he was leaving in anger, did not have a new job to go to, and could not explain exactly what was troubling him. The participant, unsure about how to respond, decided to apply the coaching method he had learned earlier that day. He started asking questions to guide the employee to answers about the real source of his issues, and to identify what he thought might relieve his anger and help him enjoy his work. After the participant spent an hour asking gentle, probing questions, without adding his own suggestions or answers, the employee realized that he needed a very short list of things to feel more empowered, engaged, and appreciated. The employee decided to stay with the company. After relating his story, the participant thanked the leader-teacher for having presented the coaching method just in time to help retain a valuable employee.

Story 2: A leader-teacher encouraged non-financial team members to be more involved in financial issues on multifunctional teams. He stated quite explicitly that non-financial people had a duty to ask questions about financial implications, and to provide input to financial team members even if that information was not requested. He then taught for a few hours on the language of finance. A week after the training, an L&D staff member sent out an email to all participants requesting feedback and stories about how they had applied what they had learned. One response contained this story: "I went to Europe for our regular multi-functional two-day team meeting. Usually, when it is time for the financial member to report, I multitask or leave to check-in with my team back home. This time I stayed and listened. I actually asked a few questions and challenged some of the assumptions. In the process, our team uncovered an issue that changed our profitability. Because I now knew enough about the financial language, and had been given a directive to work with the finance member, we were able to identify the issue and come up with a solution that strengthened our financials. It was great that we caught the issue before it was a real problem."

Story Collection Methods: Which methods were used to discover the stories you just read? Which methods might you use?

- ☐ Heard by a mentor or coach
- ☐ Part of post-event activity
- ☐ Captured as part of a knowledge-sharing exercise in a participant's own organization
- ☐ Shared as a result of a request by teaching staff
- ☐ Submitted as a report for the organization or group
- ☐ Told by participants to other leader-teachers and classmates
- ☐ Told to their managers
- ☐ Other: _____

Develop a LAT Scorecard

Sharing results for LAT programs sets the stage for taking advantage of "short-term wins." Recall, that in stage six of Kotter's Eight-Stage Change Process (see chapter 8), Kotter suggests generating visible successes and improvements. A scorecard is a great way to do that. Scorecards not only show progress, they also build credibility, and demonstrate a commitment to an ongoing program. Annual scorecards and a detailed report can help integrate your LAT approach into the culture.

The leadership in your organization may not ask for a scorecard, or any data at all. However, we recommend sending it anyway to reinforce the LAT culture. In fact, send reports regularly. Add a short cover note to summarize key conclusions, observations, and interpretations as a way to easily make the data meaningful for the reader, and to acknowledge senior leaders' usual preference for executive summaries.

Learning professionals might also choose to do return on investment (ROI) calculations. ROI analysis can be helpful at budget time. But in our experience, and according to most people we interviewed for this book, many companies don't demand ROI to validate the worth of their LAT programs. We suspect this is because they have seen, and often experienced firsthand, the value of leaders teaching.

In any case, calculating a valid ROI for a learning program, while controlling all independent variables that might also be impacting performance, is very difficult to do. Consider moving beyond ROI. Avoid getting caught up in numbers, while missing the big picture of the successful contributions that the training program has made to the business. In reality, it isn't the training program that makes the difference; the people—those who teach the content and those who put it to use on the job—are the ones who determine if programs impact performance or not.

If you need to establish some level of confidence that a learning program is driving the desired results, look into the Brinkerhoff Method. It includes doing a survey of all participants, to identify two groups—those who successfully applied the learning with dramatic results, and those who found no value in it. The next step is to analyze the major differences between the two groups. Maybe it's a difference in managers' attitudes, or the time at which the training was offered in the career of the participants. Whatever the difference, a good next step is to determine what is needed to move more participants into the successful application group. (Brinkerhoff 2003).

Alternatively, consider conducting interviews of leaders and managers—formal or informal—to get their views on the impact of the program. An especially good time for this is during the company's performance appraisal process, when the topic of performance is on everyone's mind.

We have seen that quantitative data combined with success stories, goes a long way to integrate LAT into a culture. Establishing a LAT culture requires changing habits and practices related to who teaches. Be sure to make a list of active leader-teachers available as part of a general report or to those managing leadership and executive development processes.

A regular report and scorecard for the LAT-supported program can help others see the short-term wins achieved by the LAT team. This sets you up to tackle Kotter's Stage Seven: Consolidate and Build Momentum as you prepare to expand, as discussed in the next chapter.

Check Your LAT Team's Effectiveness

Before moving to expand the LAT program, consider doing a check on the effectiveness of your LAT teams. Your LAT learning event teams and LAT initiative team are valuable resources. It's appropriate to take some time to assess the teams, their teamwork, and their results. Celebrate what is good, and set plans in place for improvement. A good time to do this is at the end of a program or program cycle when some leader-teachers are moving on to other work or other learning programs, and when it might be time to recruit some new leader-teachers. Consider using the Effective Teams model, introduced in chapter 3 and as shown in Figure 11.1, as a guide for your assessment.

Figure 11.1: Characteristics of Effective Teams

Characteristics of

Affiliation

Acculturation

Leadership

Direction

Execution

© K. Muno, 2013

Effective Teams

Affiliation—Team members know why they are part of the team, their unique roles and contributions, and how they are expected to engage and interact with others.

Direction—Each member understands and is guided by the vision, mission, goals, tasks, success criteria, timing, and resources necessary to deliver the team's results.

Execution—The team is guided by the processes needed to accomplish the tasks, such as planning, decision-making, tracking and control, and methods of meeting and communicating.

Acculturation—Team members acknowledge a culture supporting trust, celebrating success, and maintaining a focus on continual improvement and increased effectiveness over time.

Leadership—A single leader or shared leadership ensures the team is aligned to the direction, encourages inclusion, coaches to build capability, and inspires high performance to deliver results.

Learning From Leader-Teachers

"NEWLiNC is our program for new researchers from around the globe. This is a very big event covering six days and involving more than 100 people as trainers and staff. To guide and manage this program we select three Band 4 leaders who join the team of deans for three years. In year one, a dean gets to know this complex program and takes on an improvement project. In year two, a dean manages about half of the program. In year three, a dean owns half of the program and is the key moderator for the entire week. When the time comes for the year three dean to rotate out, the other deans, with the operations dean, identify several candidates who meet a three-tiered criteria: they come from a different business unit than the other two deans, the addition of the candidate continues to provide visually perceivable diversity—something highly valued by our new hires—and the candidate has professional strengths that are different from the other deans and needed for the special project identified for the next year. By having a highly diverse team, we succeed and demonstrate to new hires that this is the way P&G works."

—Jean Ibrahim, Manager (VP) R&D, Sponsor for NEWLiNC at P&G

Learn By Doing: Assessing the Effectiveness of Your LAT Team

Use the chart below to help you sort through the factors that may impact your organization's readiness levels for LAT. There are no right or wrong answers. Your responses simply reflect your understanding and assessment of the current state of readiness for LAT in your organization.

Questions	Myself	Team	Some members
Affiliation • Did team members know their role within the team? • Were roles sufficiently defined to encourage collaboration without duplication of efforts? • Did team members know who to go to with questions, ideas, or concerns? • Do we have a way to effectively integrate new members? • How do we recognize, transition, and celebrate members who leave the team?			
Direction • Is our vision/mission clear to all members? Does it need updating? • Did we have sufficient project management in place to help members know their priorities and deadlines? • Did we clearly define success in a way that helped everyone know what had to be done? • Did we have a way to manage quality and define the team's standards of success? • Did we use or establish best practices as guides for quality?			
Execution • Did team members know how to get things done? Did they know the process? • Were decisions made by the right people at the right level? • Did we have resources that we did not use? Should we try to use these resources in the future or is their value no longer relevant to our work? What resources would be helpful as we move forward? • Were our methods of communicating—meetings, mail, messages, shared files—sufficient and effective? If not, how might we improve them? • When a miscommunication occurred, did we have an effective way to get back on track? • Did we meet commitments to deliver quality on time and within budget?			
Acculturation • Did team members respect and value each other's skills, opinions, and diverse perspectives? • Was our team climate one of collaboration, or was it competitive? Cooperative or adversarial? • How did the team members react to suggestions for improvement? • Did we celebrate both big and small successes for individuals and the team?			
Leadership • Is it clear who has the final decision for each area of the program? • Did I or our team leader help or hinder member engagement? • As a leader, did I or our leader keep us focused on the ultimate goal? • Did I, or our leader help overcome barriers when these were identified?			

Responses to the above questions can help you know what to celebrate, which practices to establish as best practices, and where to place energy to improve.

The LAT Team assessment is best done on a regular basis as your team members will change over time, and multiple teams might be formed. Helping team members move to new roles can add energy to your program, and help leaders further develop their leader-teacher skills. Consider using the **progression** method (see chapter 3) of moving leader-teachers into successively more challenging or different roles in the learning programs. This also helps expand the LAT culture. As you assess the LAT team, identify who is ready to move to a different role, what new talent can be brought in, and what set of skills can be added to enhance the team and its work.

Your Turn

Jot down your thoughts on the following topics.

How might you celebrate LAT program successes? What traditions might you establish?

_____

_____

Do you want to involve leader-teachers in on-the-job application follow-up? If so, how might you do this? If not, how else can you support participants as they apply what they learned?

_____

_____

How might you get word back to leader-teachers about the impact of their teaching?

_____

_____

What measures might you use to demonstrate that the LAT initiative is contributing to the business? Will you use a scorecard? Stories? Something else?

_____

_____

How might you support the ongoing effectiveness of your LAT Teams?

_____

_____

Thinking about your organization's culture, how might you duplicate the way that the business tracks and celebrates progress and success?

_____

_____

Chapter 12

Build on Your Success

"The best way to predict the future is to create it."

—Peter Drucker

■ ■ ■

 Find Your Answers

When your LAT approach has had success, and some best practices have been established, you can begin to build on your early successes. As you read this, consider these questions:

- How will you recruit and onboard new leader-teachers?
- What process can be used to assess progress toward a LAT culture?
- How will you know when it is time to expand LAT programs, and how will you avoid common pitfalls?
- What can you learn from others to enhance your own expansion?

This chapter covers new opportunities that arise as momentum builds for LAT programs. Among the first of these opportunities is a need for more or new leader-teachers. Second, as you assess the changes in the LAT culture that have been developing, look for the next set of business challenges the LAT approach can attempt to solve. Be prepared to spot the indicators that the organization is ready to expand LAT programs—ready to go from a seed to a row, or a row to a garden.

At the end of this chapter two case studies describe different and successful LAT journeys from inception to growth.

Add New Leader-Teachers

A successful LAT process will engage enough **leader-teachers** to meet the demand while not overusing this valuable resource. The successful approach will also build a pipeline of future leader-teachers as part of an overall LAT talent management cycle of recruiting, onboarding, training, and assessment feedback. This section provides insights to help you develop your current leader-teachers and create a robust pipeline of leader-teachers for future teaching opportunities.

Find the Right Number of Leader-Teachers

How wonderful would it be to have a waiting list of leaders who want to be part of your leader-teacher program? Such success does not happen overnight. But it can happen faster than you might think if you take a step-by-step approach. Start by bringing your vision for LAT to mind. Create a list entitled "Leader-Teacher Waitlist." File it away and let everyone know that it exists. At some future date, when a leader says, "I'd be kind of interested in helping with one of these learning events," you can capture her name and interest area, and be sure not to lose this treasured resource. This is a good way to start filling the next round of leader-teacher roles.

When planning each learning program, it is helpful to recruit a team of two or three leader-teachers for each topic or program, as described in chapter 3. This provides built-in bench strength to cover any unexpected deviations from your intended delivery plans, as described in chapter 9. Two of the three candidates should have a strong grasp of the content, and the third might be a person who is being onboarded to a LAT role. By setting a standard of two or three leader-teachers per training team, it clarifies how many leader-teachers a program requires. This helps in two ways. First, it is wise not to overuse the leader-teacher as a resource. Second, a standard of two or three trainers per team helps you gently let others down when a half-dozen people volunteer to teach the same popular topic. Likewise, this standard of two or three leader-teachers per team makes it easy to identify and fill gaps in teaching teams.

For each program, consider what it means to have bench strength. Do the leaders work together to deliver a program, or do they take turns? How much of the leader's time is involved? Is it mostly advising on the design, and then participating in opening and closing remarks for a session that is delivered primarily by an external resource? Or, is it a learning event that demands full-time attention and participation for hours, or even days? The more intense the demand, the more important it is to have a solid threesome on the team. Knowing these factors can help determine the right number of leader-teachers for each program, and is good information to have available when you start recruiting new leader-teachers.

A good method for recruiting is to find the experts, those with real credibility on the topic. Ask others who they think have particularly valuable knowledge or experience to share on each topic area. Talk to managers one level above the leader-teachers you are recruiting; peers of potential leader-teachers; and others throughout the organization. As you ask around, collect stories to share with the candidate. We build confidence in our leader-teachers when we tell them, "three of your peers told me that you are the person they look to as a role model on this topic." In many instances, the candidate is unaware that they are doing so well in the eyes of others. They greatly appreciate the honest feedback and positive validation. This is true of all levels of leaders, including directors, VPs, and above.

Another method for recruiting is the **go to the light** method, described in chapter 3. Find out who has the energy and commitment for this type of work by casting a wide net for volunteers within the appropriate group of leaders. This could be because they have a deep interest in teaching or because they see a business opportunity that needs to be addressed or a problem that needs to be solved, and see teaching and learning as the answer. The more you have your ear to the ground and know your organization, the better. Another way is to simply ask for volunteers, sending out the request through formal and informal channels. You can create a sense of urgency by providing a deadline and noting that there are only two or three open spaces for each topic. This approach gives potential leader-teachers a choice of topics, and should you have more volunteers than needed, this method gives you a good start on building a waitlist. For more help on recruiting, review the book *Leaders as Teachers*.

Regardless of how you identify candidates for the leader-teacher roles, be prepared to cover these common questions described in chapter 3 of this book:

Why me? If I say "yes," what am I committing to? How does this fit into my day job?, and What is the benefit, to me and to the company?

Recruiting is easier if your LAT program already has a good reputation for supporting leader-teachers' success. A positive reputation is so important that chapters 7 through 10 all touch on building and achieving a good reputation for your program.

 Learning From Leader-Teachers

"I never learn more than when I teach. For me, teaching leadership concepts makes me a better leader. It is part of my personal leadership development program. As an HR leader, I see that the leaders who embrace teaching are our strongest leaders. Leaders who teach develop themselves while they are developing others."

—Jerry Hurwitz, Senior VP of HR, BD

Developing Existing Leader-Teachers

After a leader-teacher has delivered a topic several times, or even for several years, talk with the individual about the next teaching role or topic. The outcome of the discussion will vary depending on individual interests. Some will want to take a new role within the same program. This might include teaching one or more different modules, teaching new and updated material, or taking the lead on a section that had previously seemed too challenging to tackle as a new leader-teacher. Others may have their eye on a different program. Take advantage of any natural **progression** that develops in the program, such as teaching a similar topic at a higher level or to a demographically different group of participants.

These experienced leader-teachers may become "master teachers." These are the acknowledged go-to program leaders, and may become true experts in one or more programs. Master teachers typically become highly invested in the LAT approach and the future success of programs that they have helped develop and teach. They are also very interested in helping to develop the next generation of leader-teachers. This is a modern example of the artisan and apprentice model applied in some organizations today. This next generation of leader-teachers, with the support of a master teacher and L&D professionals, often matures in the role in a relatively short period. Providing a progression of teaching experiences can both hasten maturity in the leader-teacher role and result in additional master teachers for programs.

Preparing New Leader-Teachers

Once leaders have agreed to teach, it is the responsibility of the learning professionals to onboard and help prepare them. Onboarding for new leader-teachers has three goals:

- Assure content knowledge is sufficiently strong and focused to meet the needs of this program's learners.
- Familiarize leader-teachers with the intent, design, and agenda for the program.
- Provide support for gaining a progression of skills as a trainer or facilitator.

A walk-through of the learning event agenda and materials may address the first two items. These walk-throughs might take an hour or multiple sessions, depending on the complexity and length of the program.

The third item—trainer training—can be the toughest part because very few leaders have been taught how to train. It's important to note that some leader-teachers have good presentation skills, making others think they also will be good teachers. However, the title of the important training resource, *Telling Ain't Training*, shows that thinking to be false. It is one thing to talk at people to convey information; it is another thing to interact with participants and help them integrate new ideas and concepts in a way that will help them do things differently in the workplace. In addition, learning programs increasingly use a variety of newer technologies. Leader-teachers need guidance or support to use these tools in a way that effectively transfers knowledge from the leader-teachers to the participants. Here are some ways that others have accomplished training leader-teachers.

Quick Tip

Leader-teachers intuitively do many things well as they teach. Build confidence for your leader teachers by helping them move from unconsciously capable to consciously capable. Tell them what they do right!

Conduct a Train-the-Trainer Session

It might be a half-day session or even an external multi-day course. It's best to do this either in a small group or as individual coaching. Keep in mind that people who are operating at the top of their game may have a difficult time opening themselves up to learning a new area for which they have little knowledge or experience. Becoming a novice again takes a strong will and bravery. Minimize the chance for embarrassment.

Provide One-on-One Coaching

This is a highly recommended approach for senior executives. Personalized preparation is very time efficient, and when combined with a dose of tender loving care, is a powerful way to partner with top executives. Personal coaching for training skills builds confidence and engagement.

Have a Rehearsal

Invite a small group of staff to take the role of learners at the rehearsal. Conduct the session on location, or mock up the actual setting. Don't be surprised if the rehearsal takes twice as long as the learning event, due to discussions and helpful "do-overs." Schedule this rehearsal a minimum of one week in advance of the actual event, and preferably, even further out. This early timing provides leader-teachers space to mentally process the feedback from the rehearsal, continue preparations, and make any needed program adjustments. Leader-teachers will use the time wisely to practice and hone their grasp of the program content, and, if team-teaching, to work with their co-teachers to assure a smooth program flow.

Capture an Experienced Leader-Teacher on Video

This is best for sessions that are offered multiple times. The video helps new leader-teachers learn at a time that fits their schedule. This method is particularly helpful when a last-minute substitute is needed.

See One, Do One, Teach One

A common progression is to first experience the program as a participant, then observe and work behind the scenes with the faculty, and, as a third progression, begin to teach or co-teach an increasing number of the program modules based on their comfort level and growing expertise. This is especially effective for new leader-teachers and for those who are onboarding to a different learning program. For more difficult or new material, consider employing the success principle of "just out of reach, but not out of sight," that is, to have a master trainer near at hand to unobtrusively assist when needed.

Success Begets Success

When leader-teachers are confident and well prepared, it comes across to participants. And success begets success. It is common for participants to say something like, "I am really amazed that our leaders gave so much of their time to help us learn. How can I become a leader teacher?" These leader-teachers and master teachers help create the positive buzz about the LAT approach. They create a teaching-learning culture. When you give your leader-teachers the type of support described here, it will be no time at all until your Leader-Teacher Waitlist is multiple pages in length.

Assess Your Progress Toward a LAT Culture

Creating a LAT culture can be like defying gravity, as described in chapter 8. Give yourself a nice pat on the back if your LAT culture is growing. Culture can be an enabler for any business initiative. It can also be a very destructive force, so it is important to keep a watchful eye on the current direction of the culture. Hopefully, you have documented a few of the many LAT benefits that your business has garnered from this approach already. Now take a deeper dive to assess progress as you continue to grow your LAT culture.

 # Learn By Doing: Assess Your Progress

Read through the questions below and assess your progress to date. Use the chapter references, as needed, to help you, especially as you begin to think about next steps and new directions.

Questions	Exceeded Goals	Met Goals	Needs Improvement	Chapter Reference and Notes
Do people view LAT as important to your organization's growth or success?				Leaders as Teachers—Today's Imperative
Are you establishing your LAT plan—garden seeds, row(s), or plot—as intended?				Choose Your Starting Plan
Did your LAT team work as you expected?				Form Your LAT Team
Are you using active teaching and active learning methods with less lecture and presentations?				Design Your Active Teaching Program
Are leader-teachers practicing in the moment teaching in their day-to-day work?				Teach in the Moment
Are you tapping social networks to cause learning and collaboration on business issues?				Harness the Power of Collaborative Learning
Are employees aware of your LAT brand? Are you living up to your brand promise?				Establish Your Brand to Drive Business Results and Learning
Is momentum building to support the LAT culture and garner the benefits of LAT?				Plan for Change and Build Momentum
Are programs documented and leader-teachers prepared to support success?				Prepare for Success
Did leader-teachers feel supported and want to come back again?				Deliver With Excellence
What successes did you celebrate? How was success conveyed? Has your LAT team achieved a satisfactory level of effectiveness?				Keep Up the Momentum
Are you successfully recruiting and preparing the next round of leader-teachers and setting up LAT progression?				Build on Your Success

Based on your responses, you can make plans to further progress the LAT culture to maximize the benefits for your business.

Consider LAT Expansion

When initial LAT plans have been achieved, it may be time to expand so that your company or organization can reap more of the benefits that a LAT culture has to offer. This section offers a look at some of the indicators that it is time to expand the LAT program, along with some warnings and tips to make the journey go more smoothly.

Consider going through the Starting Point Assessment introduced in chapter 2. Has your Starting Point Assessment rating changed? If not, that is normal. Consider expanding within your current level. If you are at the Plant a Seed level, look for opportunities to plant more seeds. If at the Plant a Garden Row level, plant a few more rows. And, if at the Garden Plan level, seek out uncultivated areas. Remember, the idea here is not to get the biggest garden, but the biggest harvest from the garden you have. For each of these situations consider these elements:

- Can you still maintain the quality of the current programs while expanding?
- Have you identified best practices in the current program so that these can be intentionally reapplied to the expanded programs?
- Are you using the go to the light (chapter 3) principal as you expand?

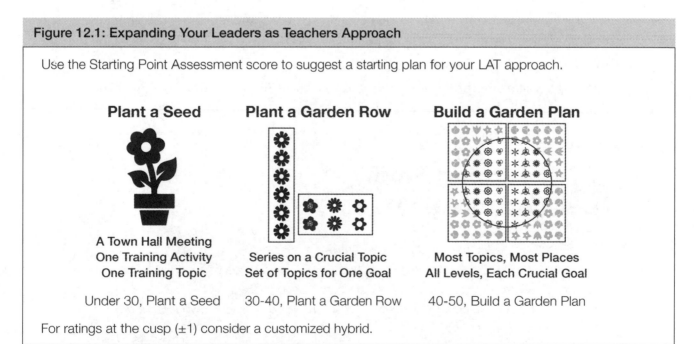

Figure 12.1: Expanding Your Leaders as Teachers Approach

Use the Starting Point Assessment score to suggest a starting plan for your LAT approach.

Plant a Seed

A Town Hall Meeting
One Training Activity
One Training Topic

Under 30, Plant a Seed

Plant a Garden Row

Series on a Crucial Topic
Set of Topics for One Goal

30-40, Plant a Garden Row

Build a Garden Plan

Most Topics, Most Places
All Levels, Each Crucial Goal

40-50, Build a Garden Plan

For ratings at the cusp (±1) consider a customized hybrid.

A jump in assessment ratings that is sufficient to cross boundaries into the next level is often driven by a combination of elements.

Learn By Doing: Rising Rating

Which of these elements might be driving a rise in the assessment rating to a new level in your organization or company?

☐ Momentum for LAT is growing among leader-teachers as more benefits are realized.

☐ LAT programs are garnering more success stories about business-relevant results.

☐ There has been a change in the business situation.

☐ There is a new or emerging business need.

How might you harness these elements to expand LAT?

_____

_____

As you consider expanding to the next level, review Figure 2.2 in chapter 2 Common Components of Varying Sizes of Learning Programs. Are you able and willing to add those things that are common for the next level up, such as an annual score card and formal train-the-trainer program for a Garden Row, or a LMS and LAT-related succession planning for a Garden Plot? Next, in chapter 2, review Figures 2.3 and 2.4 along with your own notes in that part of the chapter. Will any organizational structure changes be needed as you expand, such as staff changes to support a larger number of leader-teachers and learning events? As you expand to the next level, are there economies of scale that can be realized as you restructure? Many learning professionals related that these resources were readily available once the program was successful and the business requested a LAT expansion.

Learning From Leader-Teachers

"With the scope of day-to-day challenges that every business leader faces today, it is fair to ask where the role of teacher might stack up. I would encourage you to think about it as a top priority. Surround yourself with agile learners, spend a little time every week knowing that you shared some teachable insights, and watch your business and your team grow."

—William A Kozy, Executive VP and COO, BD

Tips and Cautions for LAT Expansion

We recommend that you grow your LAT approach in a step-by-step manner. Grow only as fast as you can while continuing to ensure success in each offering. Go slow. Go to the light. Don't over-extend. And maintain a steadfast focus on the business needs.

 Insights From Learning Professionals

"In my experience, one of the most powerful outcomes of implementing a leaders-as-teachers model is the effect on leadership engagement. The leaders who teach have the opportunity to become familiar with associates with significant future leadership potential and get to know them in a manner that would not normally occur in the business environment. The participants feel valued and engaged because senior leaders took the time out of their busy schedule to teach. The model also provides a forum for senior leadership to impart their expectations for leadership behaviors, the company culture, and the organizational strategy going forward. Capturing the hearts and minds of our future leaders is essential for the future growth of any organization."

—Nancy Allen, VP, WW Talent Management, BD

Learn By Doing: Expansion Pitfalls

The following are things that can hurt expansion. Which will you need to watch out for in your organization to assure that positive momentum continues?

- ☐ Requests to do more without a corresponding increase in resources or an innovative increase in efficiency using current resources.
- ☐ Requests to expand into areas that are not as closely connected with primary business needs.
- ☐ Expanding without taking time to assess the current or changing business situation.
- ☐ A choice to start the program with hand-selected leader-teachers, and then expanding without paying attention to potential skill development needs for new leader-teachers.
- ☐ The core program begins to falter due to outdated content, faculty weaknesses, or inadequate L&D processes and systems.
- ☐ An expansion into an organization where no LAT sponsor has yet been identified.
- ☐ Taking a successful program into a new organization without assessing differences in organizational culture, drivers, needs, and values.

How might you avoid these potential pit falls as you expand the LAT culture?

_____

_____

Case Studies of Successful LAT Expansions

Many companies interviewed for this book have successfully expanded their LAT-supported initiatives. As you read the case studies, look for commonalities with your situation, especially related to the business drivers that encouraged expansion and the approaches used to successfully expand.

SES Case Study: From Reluctant Leader-Teachers to "Sign Me Up!"

SES-Your Satellite Company, is known for its culture of pushing the boundaries of technology. Founded in 1985 in Luxembourg, as Europe's first private satellite operator, SES was on hand to deliver TV broadcasting to East Germany's 15 million viewers when the Berlin Wall fell in 1989. In the early 1990s, SES pioneered digital video broadcasting and successfully lobbied across Europe to establish DVB as the European standard. In 2004, they were the first satellite company to carry HDTV signals. So, in 2006, when Doug Clayton, senior vice president of global learning and development for human resources at SES, was asked to host an HR summit in Princeton, New Jersey, he went looking for something different, something "sort of ground-breaking and new and fresh." That's when he first learned about the **leaders-as-teachers approach**, and brought in some consultants to describe this emerging trend.

While LAT did not take root in SES following the HR Summit, the LAT concept resonated with Doug. As part of his studies with the Penn CLO Executive Doctoral Program, he appreciated an opportunity to learn more about LAT best practices.

In early 2011, SES CEO, Romain Bausch, requested a leadership curriculum for executives. Doug and the L&D team, after significant assessment and study, landed on a design that they called Momentum. It consisted of four learning modules: change readiness, SES strategy, knowledge networking, and empowerment. Doug recommended that this program be offered, not only to SES executives, but to all 1,200 employees of SES as a way to create a common vocabulary and culture for the recently restructured SES—a restructure that integrated three operating companies into one SES operation. Leadership agreed. The next step was to find an external trainer who could facilitate the program for so many people. However, the CEO had a different idea. He encouraged Doug, as a respected senior leader at SES, to teach the Change Readiness Workshop. Hence, LAT was born at SES.

Doug and his co-facilitator designed a highly interactive workshop and proceeded to teach it around the world. In the process, they began to get feedback about the progress of the recent SES organizational changes—feedback that could inform the leadership's choices. Doug and his co-facilitator shared a summary of their learning with the executive team, thereby enabling these leaders to make decisions and take action that enabled the change process to progress more smoothly. Consequently, the senior leaders saw a definite business value in the LAT approach.

Moving on to the next learning module, SES Strategy, the design team created a course on the SES strategic plan that was even more interactive than the first workshop. It included an internally designed, highly stimulating business simulation, internally produced videos, and the leaders' real life stories of their experience with strategy. Now it was time to recruit the facilitators from in-house.

Initially, some executives resisted taking on the leader-teacher role, giving comments such as, "I'm not trained to be a facilitator" or "I'm really quite busy with my full-time responsibilities, so why are you asking me to do this?" With the support of the CEO, Doug convinced the executives to trust him. After all, Doug had gone first as a leader-teacher and had learned a few things. "We will support you," he told them repeatedly.

He used a few external contractors to conduct train-the-trainer sessions for SES executives in private sessions held off-site. He did this multiple times. Slowly and patiently, he helped these leaders develop their teaching skills. And it paid off. The executives got progressively stronger and more confident in their new leader-teacher roles. Then Doug scheduled and conducted dry runs with the executives to provide practice and build confidence. Next was the pilot session, which the CEO would observe. That made some of the new leader-teachers really nervous. But they did very well! And the CEO gave immediate positive feedback.

As they delivered more workshop sessions, SES's new leader-teachers once again experienced the bi-directional benefits of LAT. Not only were participants gaining knowledge from the leader-teachers, the leaders also began to expand their framing and thinking on the topic that they were teaching—they learned what employees were feeling and thinking about the SES Strategic Plan.

For each of the Momentum workshops, 90 percent of employees attended. The employees—whether from Singapore, South Africa, Luxembourg, or North America—gave very positive feedback (an average rating of 5.6 on a 6 point scale). Their feedback revealed that they liked the activities, but, even more so, they liked to hear the real life stories told by leader-teachers.

The leader-teachers themselves became converts to the LAT approach. They were learning things, as exemplified by this story Doug shared, "We typically did a group reflection at the end of each session, where we would ask participants something simple such as, 'name one thing that you got out of the session today,' 'what worked for you,' or 'what didn't work for you.'"

And it was usually very positive feedback. During one of these feedback sessions, the participants thanked Daniel Biedermann, senior vice president of corporate development at SES for being there and for teaching. Daniel said, "I want to thank you! It was a privilege to stand here and share today's session with you. I thought I was going to teach you, but, indeed, you helped me see our SES strategic plan from your point of view, and that will help me in the future. Thank you."

Doug tells us. "That was powerful: The strategy expert learning from the people he was teaching about strategy! And to think that at the beginning, Daniel was one of those reluctant leader-teachers. With a thoughtful, introverted communication style and very little experience with facilitating, I might have been tempted to give him a pass on being a leader-teacher. I'm glad I didn't. Daniel did an excellent job in the workshop. He ended the day with 'Thank you. You taught me a lot.' I'll never forget that."

And the expansion of the LAT approach continues. In January 2013, the CEO asked the L&D group to design a course on IT Security, that is, on how to protect the company from cyber attacks and such things. "This training is just as important to me as the strategy training was," the CEO told Doug. So the L&D team went back to the well of leaders-as-teachers.

The success of the first round of courses led to a favorable attitude toward LAT. This time it was much easier when Doug went to recruit a team of high-level IT managers to create content. He continued to apply best practices from the previous workshops. First, to develop facilitation skills SES used train-the-trainer sessions and a pilot. Second, the course design was very interactive with videos and exercises. One day, one of the IT security leader-teachers stopped Doug in the hallway to thank him for insisting that he take on the role of leader-teacher. "I really didn't want to do that, but once we got into it, it was so interactive, it was great fun. Anytime you have a class for me to teach, you can sign me up," the IT leader told Doug. Again, it was a big success.

With one LAT success after another, Doug tells us, "This is now the way we do training. We have more than 20 leader-teachers at SES! And the phrase leaders as teachers is part of our culture."

Banner Health Case Study: On Becoming a Net Exporter of Leaders as Teachers

Since its inception in 1999, Banner Health has used the leaders-as-teachers approach. "We haven't had external speakers or facilitators for most training. We've been fortunate enough to have a pool of great talent within our organization to deliver our leadership programs," says Jerry Lewis, program director of talent optimization.

"In 2005, we started recruiting our leaders to teach. And in 2008, we launched our Leadership Symposiums as a new way to offer our leadership classes. The LAT approach became more structured. These symposiums were like breakout sessions at large conferences. They were a week long, with classes starting at 8 a.m. and some running into the evening each day. Participants were able to pick and choose which classes they would like to attend throughout the week. The attendance averaged between 1,000 and 1,400 leaders for each symposium held in Arizona," he said. With Banner Health having 24 facilities located in seven states, a total of 12 Leadership Symposiums were held each year—four in Arizona, four in Colorado, two in Alaska, and two in Nevada. All of the symposiums were taught by BH leaders. At first it was easy to recruit leader-teachers. "We would put out an 'all call,' and the response was tremendous," Jerry recalls. "The learning team would pair leaders up with courses based on their interests, expertise, experiences, and their experience with facilitating."

Three years later, BH starting having required courses for leaders at various levels. This changed things. Already, some of the more than 200 leader-teachers were feeling handcuffed to their course after three years with no one to take over for them. Behind the scenes, there was a bit of begging going on in order to get leader-teachers to put the classes on their schedules. The long-term view for the symposiums was not looking good. Michael Abrams, then a leader-teacher for one of the learning programs that Jerry was coordinating, got the inside scoop. "We do have some leaders who are just passionate and wonderful presenters, exactly like you would want them to be," Michaels said, yet others seemed to be teaching out of a sense of duty. Some were very skilled in facilitation, others, not so much.

In 2010, Michael took on a new leadership role as senior director of talent optimization, which included Jerry's area of responsibility. Michael soon learned of an emerging need. It was becoming apparent to BH senior leaders that many of the newer leaders and mid-level leaders lacked executive presence, good communication skills, and experience with leading effective meetings.

Michael saw this as a great opportunity and jumped right on it. "Let's attack this differently," he said. "Let's make leaders as teachers a certification program. So, it's not something that we recruit you for, or beg and plead with you to become a part of, but rather we make it a development program. So instead of us taking something from you, saying 'come do this for us,' we flipped it and said, 'here's a new leadership development program aimed at leaders who want to develop executive presence, facilitation skills, public speaking, and such.'"

Michael, Jerry, and the learning team established a Leaders as Teachers Certification (LATC) process that would teach a set of standard competencies for facilitators. The goal was to start with the 200 leader-teachers first, and, in the future, have certification as a requirement for teaching classes in the Leadership Academy, which was the next iteration of the Leadership Symposium. After that, Michael and Jerry planned to actively market the program to the HR folks and to the leadership community for those leaders who were identified or nominated as candidates through Banner Health's Talent Management Review Process.

There were several steps in the process to get LAT-certified. Michael explains, "You would be recruited to go through the certification. You would go through a series of courses on facilitation, along with programs on executive presence, good communication, and leading effective meetings. You pick a style of facilitation—a training modality to specialize in, either traditional, live-virtual, blended, or experiential—and train in that style. You would have an executive advisor, and get an evaluation to tell you what area of facilitation you need to grow in. In the end, they 'owe us' a certain number of hours as a facilitator to complete their LATC." These "owed" hours provided newly certified leader-teachers with an opportunity to practice, hone, demonstrate, and receive additional feedback on their new skills.

Once again the Leadership Academy had a full pipeline of leader-teachers to train the program. And the quality of the facilitation was up! Additionally, the leader-teachers really wanted to be there, because, as Michael explains, "instead of taking something away from them, they are getting something."

This idea of "raising the bar" on the quality of leader-teacher facilitation had dramatic effects. Leadership effectiveness data is available on each department, so there is real evidence of the change in leader effectiveness before and after the training. Ed Oxford, VP and chief talent officer, noticed what a difference the LATC made, and asserted that only those leaders with LATC should be making presentations to the executive committee.

There are now more than enough leader-teachers to staff the leadership development courses. While many of the new LATC leaders teach their required hours and move on, others want to continue to use these new skills. So now, LATC has become a feeder pool of talented facilitators for other parts of the organization. Michael explains, "So, once a leader gets in and certified, you start to get a list of opportunities that go well beyond the learning team." For example, the service excellence team has requested LATC leaders to facilitate their customer service training. The learning team has become an exporter of leader-teachers!

With LATC, there are so many leader-teachers who have learned to facilitate in non-traditional modalities of training—live virtual, blended, and experiential—that Michael and Jerry were able to transition the costly traditional style Leadership Symposiums to online and virtual. Now those leaders in states other than Arizona are no longer at a disadvantage. Everyone has equal access to great training, and at a reduced cost. And Banner Health's LATC leaders are fully prepared and capable to lead each session.

Naturally, with so many leader-teachers, there is a team that is vital to their support. The Strategic Program Alignment (SPA) Team creates the materials, manages logistics, books classrooms, books online classes, sets up meeting schedules, schedules the leader-teachers, arranges for co-facilitators to meet in advance of a course, and procures all the facilitator and participant materials. The transition from teaching live classes to virtual learning approaches for leadership training freed up time for the SPA team.

With the virtual leadership classes running smoothly, Michael felt that the learning team could lend a hand to help with New Employee Orientation (NEO). Due to the company's continued growth, the organization that managed the NEO program was beginning to get overwhelmed. Every Monday morning, 100 to 150 newly hired employees participate in NEO. The participants range from receptionists to nutritionists to doctors. The program was a two and a half hour Power-Point presentation. Michael and Jerry reshaped the program into a 45-minute experiential course. At first, people were skeptical that a program without Power-Point would work. Indeed, with a less skilled leader-teacher, they learned that it didn't work very well. However, with LATC in place, and with only those certified in the experiential modality doing the teaching, the course has become a wonderful common experience that all new employees share.

The learning team offers a half day Quarterly Up-Skills Session to help leader-teachers continue to improve. Both Michael and Jerry continue to teach and co-facilitate as they broaden the skill set of the organization's leaders.

Not only was the learning team exporting leader-teachers to other training programs throughout the company, developing leaders, and staffing NEO, but when the need arose for teaching the course, Language of Caring—the holy grail of patient experience measures—Banner Health's leaders, with their LATC in hand, were fully ready to take on this program as well.

Your Turn

Jot down your thoughts on the following topics.

What ideas have you read about that could help you assure a sufficient number of leader-teachers to meet the LAT needs of your business? (Also see chapter 3.)

_____

_____

With the LAT culture evolving, how might you take advantage of positive momentum to embed LAT and LAT benefits further into the culture? (See chapter 8.)

_____

_____

What indicators are present (or will you look for) to suggest that it may be time to expand the LAT approach?

_____

_____

As you expand, what program improvements might you add? What new infrastructure or systems might be needed? (See chapter 2.)

_____

_____

Was there something in these case studies that you might build on for your own LAT program expansion?

_____

_____

Chapter 13

Get Inspired By LAT Success Stories

"Success is about creating benefit for all and enjoying the process. If you focus on this and adopt this definition, success is yours."

—Kelly Kim

■ ■ ■

Find Your Answers

Consider these questions as you read the case studies.

- What do you think drove success in each of these stories?
- Would you like to replicate the success of any of these cases? What would it take to make it happen?
- What success story would you like to be able to tell about your LAT culture and initiatives?

This chapter shares some of the stories from other companies who are successfully using the leaders-as-teachers process. Their stories inspired us, and we hope they inspire you too. These stories are from the following companies: BD, Boeing, HP, Merck, P&G, and Signature Health. See chapter 12 for cases from Banner Health and SES, as well as the many shorter stories from these companies and others throughout the chapters of this book.

Benefits of BD's Leaders-as-Teachers Approach Increase as the Program Expands

The successful leaders as teachers program at BD (Becton, Dickinson, and Company), a global manufacturer of medical supplies and devices, took shape in 2000 when former CEO Ed Ludwig turned to then chief learning officer Ed Betof and team to design and implement a corporate university featuring leaders as faculty. The two Eds have since retired from BD, but the LAT approach they instituted continues to add value to the company and evolve in new and different ways to address business and talent needs, and growth opportunities.

Like most companies, BD went through a belt-tightening exercise in response to the financial crisis from 2007 to 2009. Deb Wijnberg, worldwide leadership development and learning leader/talent management, said her team turned to technology and a blended approach to assuage the ever-increasing thirst for knowledge and interaction with company leaders, given their smaller budget.

One highlight of their technology-enabled approach is a series of 90-minute leader-led webinars on topics identified by a needs assessment survey of mid-career, high potential talent around the globe. The series features lectures on topics likely to impact BDs strategy and future performance, including:

- organic innovation, and moving promising projects through BD's innovation funnel
- impact of the new Affordable Care Act on the markets BD serves
- underlying economics of healthcare and the concepts of out-comes-based medicine.

Whether 90-minute sessions are facilitated by company leaders or outside experts, leader-teachers, known as mentoring advisors, support each session to situate the content in BD's specific context.

Deb says a rigorous process to select these faculty means the team of leader-teachers requires very little training or preparation.

"We are carefully selecting these individuals," Deb says. "They are typically leaders at a mid-level and up in the company. We know that they are very articulate; they're certainly subject matter experts in the areas that they are asked to represent.

"As a matter of their normal course of doing business in their real jobs, their day jobs, they have to work virtually with people all the around the globe all the time."

"And they are passionate and are highly motivated," adds Nancy Allen, VP of talent management, learning, and development. "They have so much infectious energy that it takes very little for us to have to guide them, and help them be successful."

The addition of technology to the teaching opportunity mix for leaders adds to the value of leaders' teaching experiences. Deb Wijnberg says leaders now praise the program for helping them get their messages to broader audiences and for introducing them to a new technology platform, in addition to the value of deepening their own understanding of the topics they teach.

Leaders at the top of BD still teach, often by conducting town hall meetings to share insights on company direction and fielding questions. Their direct reports, and leaders two levels below the C-suite, regularly teach in the classroom in two leadership programs: Leading Growth and Innovation and Creating Shared Value.

Leader-teachers also serve as sponsors of action learning projects, and participate "shoulder-to-shoulder" with experts from consulting firms like PDI, a Korn Ferry Company, to review assessment results with leaders in the general management, mid-career, and early-career leadership accelerator programs. They listen to practice sessions for presentations that program participants will make to senior leaders to share work they've completed on course projects.

Leader-teachers also play an important role in the profiling assessments BD conducts. Leaders facilitate all aspects of the strategic profiling methodology to analyze a business opportunity or performance issue from multiple perspectives—competitors, customers, and product mix—and to collaboratively develop recommendations for the business unit or team that raised the issue and requested support. They similarly lead and facilitate organizational profiling projects. In both types of assessments, leaders must learn to acquire the information from the analysis, and then filter and teach it to other leaders to support the development of recommendations, and the eventual implementation of those recommendations.

Deb and Nancy noted that BD's leaders-as-teachers program is also meeting a new need to find good talent deeper in the organization.

"It serves as an engagement tool, and is also serving as a talent development tool for us as we start brokering talent across the businesses, and leaders are getting to know folks who are out there who aren't necessarily in their own businesses," Nancy said.

"They're engaging face-to-face with talent that they may not have been exposed to in their day jobs because they may work in a different worldwide business, a different function, and even in a different region or location," adds Deb.

Boeing Builds More Than Aircraft: Boeing Builds Leaders

As you enter the Boeing Leadership Center in St. Louis, you cannot help but notice the wall of photographs of Boeing leaders. On closer investigation, it becomes clear that these are not leaders of the past, but leaders of the present. Under each photo is a quote. If you come back at a different time, you might see a fresh set.

John Messman and Brian Parker explained that these are just some of Boeing's senior leaders, all of whom serve as leaders teaching leaders, or LTLs. There are so many that they have to rotate the photos on a regular basis. John, Boeing's director of leadership development, tells us, "The wall, well, it's inspiring. The quotes are by the leaders themselves on the leadership attributes that they teach and model. The quotes emphasize the credibility these people have in their chosen topic area."

Boeing has six leadership attributes that are used to measure the performance of every Boeing leader: charts the course, sets high expectations, inspires others, finds a way, lives Boeing values, and delivers results. These attributes are fundamental to the management model that Boeing follows as it works to build leaders for its future in addition to aircraft, satellites, and so much more in the commercial, defense, and space industry for customers across the globe.

Leadership attributes is just one of the many areas taught by LTLs in the company's leadership development programs. Other areas include managing the business, managing and coaching employee performance, innovation, global mindset, creating value, diversity and inclusion, and influence and engagement for the informal leader. Most programs are organized by level—new, first-level, mid-level, executive, and high-potentials.

More than 3,500 LTL sessions have been taught in Boeing Leadership Development programs since 2007, with about a third of these being taught outside the brick and mortar walls of the Learning Center. More than 6,000 managers come through the Leadership Center each year, where they interact with Boeing's LTLs.

"LTL was [Boeing chairman, president, and CEO] Jim McNerney's idea," John explains. "He'd been in a number of top leadership positions across several different industries before he came to Boeing, and all of those experiences influenced his thinking. His guidance is that external subject matter experts typically know their theory but do not necessarily know every company well, but Boeing's own leaders bring both leadership expertise and a deep knowledge of the company's real-world challenges and opportunities—and teaching tests the leaders, too."

For the past several years, leadership development has leveraged a unique Leaders Teaching Leaders methodology that they design into their learning programs. Here is how it works:

"Each of our VPs teach two leadership classes a year at minimum, with at least one being taught at the Leadership Center," says Brian, a key member of the leadership development team. "This is a part of each leader's annual performance assessment. But many teach more than that. Some senior leaders teach up to 10 times a year or more. Each VP picks the topic and time, based on their interest and schedule. Leadership development program leaders work with the VPs to shape their message and technique, and afterwards provide a critique of their delivery as part of continuous improvement."

The unique part of Boeing's program is the three key tenets of their LTL methodology:

- dialog, not monologue
- ask challenging questions
- tell compelling stories.

These three tenets yield learning programs in which, as Brian describes, "participants hear from Boeing leaders who share their own compelling stories, in a listen-and-learn interactive forum, how their leadership experience links to Boeing's overall goals and strategies. Participants are encouraged to question and challenge those leaders, absorbing the experience and taking it back to their own organizations where they become the teacher, employing the Boeing LTL methodology. In the end, this creates a continuous learning environment where everyone is both a learner and a teacher at all levels. That's the key to opening Boeing's culture and building the atmosphere where everyone can succeed. Since there's a direct connection between learning and leading, Boeing relies on its leadership teams to drive the leadership spirit throughout the enterprise.

"To help our executives learn how to deliver a leaders teaching leaders module, we provide multiple resources, including a website that we call LTL in Action," Brian explains. "Here they learn from experienced LTLs who answer questions in recorded interviews and demonstrate the Leaders Teaching Leaders Methodology in video excerpts from actual classroom training. These videos are open for all to see."

Having this online reference is an important element for a culture that strives to build leaders. Each manager who attends a leadership development program is encouraged to "use the LTL methodology when they return home, so we get a cascade-down approach," Brian says. "Given that maximizing learning across the enterprise is foundational to our management model, it's the job of a leader to teach, and teach others how to teach within the departments that they lead."

The methodology is intended to provide two-way learning. A robust pre/during/post process ensures success and learning for LTLs and participants alike. "It is understood that the LTLs are here to learn, just as much as the participants," Brian explains.

John sums it up, "leaders teaching leaders is how we grow the capability and competencies of our organization, and part of leadership is about us developing ourselves. Leaders teaching leaders is not telling participants what to do,

- It's about engaging, growing, and stretching your people—it's about leaders building the next leaders of the Boeing Company.
- It's about taking risks and letting discussions flow freely while staying focused on inspiring performance and leveraging the best of Boeing.

- It's about engaging participants in stimulating dialog and, when necessary, taking them to the edge of their comfort zone.
- It's about how you will challenge them to demonstrate strategic thinking and solving real problems in real time right before your eyes when there are no easy solutions."

When managers step into Boeing's Leadership Center, they travel past the LTL wall of inspirational quotes, reminding them that they are about to learn from leaders and that they themselves are expected to be leaders-teaching-leaders. Boeing, a blue chip company with more than 170,000 employees, is building leaders and setting an example for the world.

Fathers of HP Would Be Pleased to See Their Founding Principles Alive in Leader-Teachers

Bill Hewlett and David Packard started the multibillion-dollar technology giant, HP, in a one-car garage and on a set of principles they called The HP Way, a philosophy that champions openness, honesty, and organization flexibility.

Meg Whitman, formerly of eBay fame and now CEO at HP, preserved The HP Way core values that contributed to the company's 75-year record of success, but simplified 21 leadership competencies to five leadership attributes, and last December launched a refreshed culture model, the "HP Way Now." Other core principles and a new rallying cry were added to create an ecosystem that would unify a very diverse corporate culture as One HP.

When Mark Bocianski, senior vice president of global talent and organization development, arrived at HP after having served as chief talent officer for the newly merged AON-Hewitt, one of his first efforts centered on implementing a career-stages program. These efforts involve HP leaders as talent developers and teachers in a variety roles and approaches.

"We wanted the curriculum for leadership development to span the entire lifecycle of an employee. So we have something for individual contributors something for managers, something for executives, and something for senior executives," Mark notes. HP also instituted accelerated development programs for high potential talent.

A branding campaign assigned names to leadership programs that described the aims of leaders at each level. Emerge is an accelerated development program for individual contributors. Engage is a program targeted to managers. Derived from the notion that employees don't quit companies, they quit bosses, HP's program for managers emphasizes their responsibility to engage teams. Director-level leaders participate in the Align leadership program to highlight their mission to align the organization with the company's strategy. Executives at HP include directors and vice presidents who attend the Inspire program to develop them as inspirational leaders. The Unite program develops the firm's most senior executives who are facilitating unity under One HP.

Mark says the next step is to put a core program in place that will extend a leadership development program to the entire remaining HP population. "Our fundamental belief is that everyone needs to have leadership development."

HP leaders support the tiered leadership development programs through varied teaching, coaching, and mentoring roles. Mark says there's an expectation that leaders will get involved.

"I think about mentoring and sponsorship, and coaching for that matter, as a continuum. And we have informal mechanisms, and we have more formal mechanisms, and then we have highly customized mechanisms," he said.

For example, one leadership development program targeted a group of 25 high potential women. Twenty-five senior leader sponsors each selected one program participant as a protégé. Meg Whitman served as executive sponsor for the program.

"We provided quite a bit of upfront training to both the sponsors and the protégés and then brought them together for a face-to-face meeting to walk through some additional context," Mark explained.

HP specifically distinguishes sponsors from mentors because the role of sponsors goes further. Sponsors received guides to conduct prescriptive dialogs about the aspects of participants' jobs that will make a difference to the organization.

Sponsors become deeply familiar with protégés capabilities and work products throughout the 18-month relationship, and can therefore, effectively and meaningfully advocate protégés to other senior leaders.

"The expectation from a measurement perspective is that we're actually going to see opportunities over the course of the 18 months, presented to these 25 women, that will represent a career move up one level. And so we're going to be tracking to see what kind of roles they end up taking that are as a direct result of the sponsor playing an active part in that process," he said.

Some HP functions have also been using Triple Creek to help find suitable matches between mentors and mentees. The Triple Creek solution is about to be extended across the entire HP enterprise. Other formal mentoring programs span an 18-month period that formally guides and tracks monthly meetings between mentors and mentees.

HP also recently launched a seven-month, five-module program with Harvard University focused on HP's leadership competencies, and a nine-month program on innovation with Stanford University.

Both programs feature a new segment of content each month, and a different HP leader is assigned to support each topic by helping to weave the company's and the external market's context "into the fabric of the program."

"So they're listening to the webinars by the Harvard faculty, or Stanford faculty. They're participating in the discussion forums, and they're facilitating the context session, which happens towardsthe end of that month," Mark said.

According to Mark, two benefits are already apparent. The high potential population gets very important exposure to senior leaders, and senior leaders relish the opportunity to leverage high potential talent and their knowledge and expertise. "So it's good on both fronts."

Leaders also present to onboarding programs for other leaders. The chief strategist facilitates discussions on company strategy in an executive onboarding program.

"One of our leadership competencies is 'people developer.' So there is an expectation that you are going to develop your people on your team. Now that takes a variety of forms," Mark said.

HP is formalizing its development planning process to ensure that every employee has a personal development plan. HP also is implementing Workday, a human capital management, finance, and analytics application, to capture significantly more information about HP talent.

"That's going to give us a whole lot capability to not only capture the kind of information that today sits in multiple systems, but it also gives us the ability to have some pretty sophisticated analytics," Mark said.

Sounds like Bill Hewlett and David Packard would be quite pleased to see how the founding principles they established more than seven decades ago continue to be put into action by leaders dedicated to finding and keeping the best talent available.

Merck Makes Magic With Leader-Teachers By Finessing Four Simple Ideas

Merck's business is growing, yet challenged by both internal and external forces around the world. Sharon Moshayof, talent development leader for global markets at Merck (known as MSD outside the United States and Canada), has to get leaders ready to keep up with the firm's fast-growing emerging markets region. (According to a second quarter, 2013 earnings report, emerging markets accounted for 22 percent of Merck's revenues, and China demonstrated especially strong performance.)

Sharon and others who design leadership programs at Merck, seem to have hit on a winning formula that puts the leaders-as-teachers approach at its core. The formula starts with four very basic ideas:

- Blend external expertise (academic faculty or other experts) with internal perspectives from Merck leaders who share real-world experiences.
- Work with leaders to make it personal.
- Invest ample time identifying the best leaders and matching them to the right topics.
- Keep it simple.

Perhaps it's nothing that you haven't heard dozens of times, yet Merck's magic evolves through the execution.

Blend External and Internal Expertise

First, consider the subtleties Merck adds to make the external and internal blend work. To teach basic business acumen, Merck invites the CFO or a regional finance leader and pairs them with an outside expert on finance. One of the key success factors, she says, is having this internal-external collaboration team meet before they teach to share models and frameworks, and become familiar with each other's message.

"One reinforces external best practice and models, and the other says, 'And here's how this plays out in Merck, and here's how you might want to think about it when you engage with business issues.'"

As Sharon was developing an Emerging Markets Future Leaders (EMFL) program to build entrepreneurial mindsets and encourage risk-taking, it became obvious that the "blended" approach was the way to go. She partnered with Harvard Business Publishing (HBP) to source expert faculty, and then assigned Merck leader-teachers, one per module. The president of Emerging Markets for Global Human Health (GHH) took a lead role and was one of the first leaders as teachers on the program.

"While the external lecturer, the Harvard person, was delivering a module, I would have our internal person on the webinar not just as a participant, but really, as a panelist," she said. "So it showed up very integrated to our participants."

Most of the leadership programs emphasize leaders teaching. Here are a few examples.

- Merck CEO Ken Frazier invited high potentials to participate in a program where Merck leaders made up 80 percent of the faculty.
- An executive development program teams up Merck leader-teachers with professors from Wharton who serve as program facilitators.
- A people management program for frontline supervisors features the managing director for Canada sharing his people management stories and experiences.

In the leadership space, Sharon says she can't think of a single program that doesn't incorporate a LAT approach. "It gives you that role modeling, that very pragmatic personal experience, and again, where you blend it with best practice from outside in terms of a Harvard- or a Wharton-level teaching faculty, I think then you've really got the best of both worlds."

Make It Personal

On the second basic point of their success model—helping leaders make it personal—Sharon works one-on-one with leaders over the phone about four weeks before they will teach to encourage them to focus on personal stories and experiences rather than on the traditional heavy PowerPoint approach.

"Leaders love it. If we had said, 'You need to come to a one-week course to learn how to be a leader-teacher,' it would never have happened," Sharon explains.

During one-on-one calls, Sharon coaches leader-teachers, saying, "What you want to be doing is having a conversation, telling your stories, and engaging people." She hopes to move from teaching "about" a topic like strategy to telling personal examples of their efforts to develop strategies—sharing what worked, what didn't, and where pitfalls emerge.

Sharon encourages leaders to think about how they themselves learn. "It's got to be memorable," she says, "Tell your story. You don't need to get a PhD in education to be able to do a good job here. Just be a leader as teacher."

Her prompting works. She said leaders' stories suggest that it's okay to make mistakes, and that it's important to take risks. "When they make it personal, when they share their journeys, when they share what's made them who they are today, that's when I think the learners are in a real 'sit-up-and-pay-attention' mode."

Beyond storytelling, leaders also are encouraged to model what they're teaching. Taking risks and developing an entrepreneurial mindset required sharing examples of learning from failure. Leaders walked a fine line. "How do you show up as, on the one hand, knowledgeable, but at the same time, vulnerable and surviving mistakes?"

She said they performed superbly. "Humility shown by leaders was incredibly powerful. We were able to send some really, really great messages."

Match Talent to Topic

On the third basic step in the formula, Sharon has discovered success factors for selecting the right leaders.

"Not every leader is going to be naturally good at this. So I sat with the senior-most leader and said, 'Who would we want to think about approaching for these modules?'"

She then introduces the idea by telling the candidates they were recommended for the teaching role. "They find it very flattering and it appeals to their need to show up in this way, to get a lot of positive reinforcement from their peers, their bosses, and the rest of the organization," she explains.

Sharon also selects leaders who are comfortable using virtual meeting technology. "Everything I'm talking about is global so very little of what we're doing at the moment is in a classroom," she notes. Many Merck leaders have a good comfort level using the technology because a majority of meetings with virtual teams have moved online.

"They all have webcams. They join, they have their slides running on the side. They have their own selves on video. They have people chatting in questions, raising hands, telling leaders to go faster, slower, clapping, smiling."

Keep It Simple

Merck's final success idea about keeping it simple shows up in all aspects of their programs: program designs, leader preparation, and evaluations.

"We make it bite-sized for them and we make success easy, and then when they see how well-appreciated it is, they just want to do more," she says.

To demonstrate how much leader-teacher sessions are appreciated, Sharon ensures that leaders receive immediate feedback by sharing the results of a simple three-question survey, which participants complete at the end of a course.

Great successes always live in the finer points of execution. It's the attention to detail that often sets apart great programs from the uninspired ones. That's why Merck's current leadership development programs are getting great reviews.

"We're getting a lot of tremendous, tremendous feedback. Very positive," Sharon says. "The leaders who participate in the programs appreciate having their own leaders as teachers. It isn't an 'either/or.' It is both."

Merck's approach that puts leaders-as-teachers at its core has been applauded externally as well. The Emerging Markets Future Leaders program was awarded

Gold in the Global Learning category at the CLO Learning in Practice awards in 2013.

Beyond the accolades, Merck is seeing an emergent benefit they never expected. In one program in the Asia-Pacific region, the cohort in the program decided to teach themselves the third segment of the course. "What's important," says Sharon, "is just the mindset of a group of leaders who have seen their own leaders showing up as teachers, and are now saying, 'Hey, we are leaders. We can actually teach each other.'"

Through a perfect example of role modeling, Merck's next generation of leader-teachers are finding themselves.

Benefits of P&G's Leaders as Teachers Approach Increase as the Program Expands

If you heard that a company had hundreds of "volunteer" leader-teachers, would you be tempted to roll your eyes in disbelief? How about discovering that people in business units with a passion for a given topic own responsibility for courses in the corporate curriculum—not the folks assigned on the HR learning team?

Feeling skeptical about anything this crazy actually working?

That, indeed, is the formula for corporate learning at one of the most successful companies in the world—Procter & Gamble (P&G). The model has emerged since the company began in 1837. With a track record of increasingly greater success for more than 176 years, something about the model must work really well.

The culture formed long ago.

"When the company was smaller, people would sit around big tables and share what they learned about the business," says Ricky Mathews, global product supply learning and development leader. "I think over time this has been sort of a consistent cultural heritage and gives us a ton of benefit."

"Storytelling is built into this culture," says Ann Schulte, P&G's global leader of learning and development (L&D). Over time, P&G has put structures in place to prompt, encourage, and support this propensity for leaders to teach. But before you look at the tactics behind how it works, you must peer deeper into the culture of P&G to get a glimpse at why it works.

P&G leaders don't just think of what they do as teaching or training. They are helping people develop and solve problems.

"If you can help people be competent, then you're going to help them become confident, which helps them make improved contributions which then gives them courage. So, there's an evolution," says Ricky.

He explains it this way. "If you align me on the mission and get me energized, you're going to get more than a minimal effort because my energy will now go toward figuring out how to deliver that mission in the best way. That might mean I'll pull capabilities from online resources, other people, or other firms, because now I have an understanding of what we're trying to accomplish."

"The what in these learning scenarios is not the content of a training program. The what becomes the level and types of contributions leaders can inspire in people. The mindset turns to action in this way: When a P&G manufacturing team ships out products with a challenging deadline or avoids a potential quality incident, the first thing leaders say is, 'Let me take accountability for codifying what we did to get the right capability in place. And now, let's talk about how we accomplished this so that we can be ready for the next challenge,'" he said.

"This is a company where managers truly accept the responsibility to develop their people," Ann adds. "I've never really seen managers, on a consistent basis, up, down, and across the organization, take responsibility for growing their people like I've seen here."

"The culture reinforces itself," says Mecislavs Maculevics, sr. HR manager, L&D, who described what it was like to experience this style of leadership as a junior employee. "I've had the benefit of switching continents and countries within P&G, and seeing the behavior that gets rewarded through promotions and visibility. You start to associate investing in people, investing in capability, as a key to success."

The dedication to developing talent emanates from P&G's "build-from-within" culture.

"P&G has always been focused on building, or promoting, our leaders from within," Fred Roneker, sr. HR manager L&D, notes. "Developing strong leaders is necessary for our company to thrive, and frankly, to survive. As a build-from-within company, we absolutely must grow and develop people because we're counting on those people to become the company's next-generation of leaders." The developing talent philosophy truly adheres to the 70:20:10 framework that suggests people learn best when 70 percent of their development relates to challenging work assignments, 20 percent to the social aspects of learning such as coaching and mentoring, and 10 percent occurs through formal learning programs.

It's not unusual for people to begin to wonder if they're receiving training when they aren't routinely going off-site to attend programs, and much of the learning happens on the job. Ann says the company is improving its communication to help people recognize the learning and development opportunities they experience in new work assignments.

P&G has won many accolades and awards for learning and leadership development programs. Ann says that as an experienced hire, joining the firm just two years ago, she was able to quickly highlight how effective P&G's approach has been and relate it to the popular 70:20:10 philosophy. "I was able to reinforce for them the heritage of 'development through experience' that has built this great business, which in turn made it easier to propose some new ideas for continuous improvement.

"We've refreshed curricula and introduced the P&G Leadership Academy to integrate leadership offerings with functional curricula, eliminating some duplication that existed," she says.

Her team also must develop the teaching and facilitation skills of the volunteer training force. Because storytelling is a key element of leaders' teaching approaches, the L&D team includes a storytelling workshop for middle managers and senior leaders in the P&G Leadership Academy.

Today, L&D is working to move some programs, and their leader-teachers, to virtual, collaborative, learning environments to better meet the needs of a truly global workforce. Their first success was a senior leader program partnering with Harvard Business School Publishing and delivered with Harvard's collaborative online platform. "Our leaders were very excited with a program that allowed exposure to thought leaders as well as connection with each other in a remote environment, just 90 minutes a week," says Amanda Lutz, HR manager, L&D.

Amanda manages the learning technology platforms for the organization and is building an internal virtual platform similar to the Harvard system.

"Our virtual platform should allow us to reach learners in a much more timely manner. We should be able to run more sessions, in smaller groups, more frequently, and without the travel expense," she says. L&D has to drive the success of the online platform. The team is now working to teach leaders-as-teachers how to interact with learners in the online platform; how to stimulate online discussion, become virtual coaches and cheerleaders, and help drive accountability so that people are completing self-guided activities. They also engaged an expert from the higher education world to teach the team and facilitators how to be effective online. "We have long required our volunteer trainers to take a course we call HIT-D (High Impact Training Delivery)" says Ann. "With our new methods we have created a virtual companion course called HIT-V. It only makes sense that we would provide the same level of skill development for online instructors as we do for the classroom."

The P&G team agrees that if you have leaders come into the learning environment, by any means, to just "inject knowledge" and then leave, the learning benefits quickly evaporate. Ann says, "If the leaders don't reinforce the learning through their daily work, their monthly reviews, their quarterly interaction, and their one-to-ones, then that injection quickly fades. Anything we teach, the leader has to be experienced in that concept. When they've had experience doing it, their credibility really accelerates adoption."

All of these efforts are leading to a reinforcement of continuous learning in the culture. Leaders and teams are beginning to talk about more than the learning programs people attend or the work that goes into helping them grow. They talk about measures of success, getting results faster, building an environment of trust, and why attaining improvements means more coaching.

The conversations are inspiring and a culture of leaders as teachers is supporting a more holistic evolution to a culture of learning.

Signature Health CEO: The Quintessential Leader-Teacher

Leaders often say that people are the company's most important asset. But few "walk the talk" quite like Joe Steier, president and CEO of Signature Healthcare, a leading provider of long-term care, rehabilitation, and healthcare services operating in seven states in the east and southeast regions of the United States.

Joe followed a path that most business leaders do, earning a bachelor's degree and taking on sequential responsibilities as he moved up the leadership ladder. And, like most business leaders, he eventually earned an MBA.

But Joe learned early something many leaders are just now learning, and others have yet to learn. He saw that value in business was shifting toward a balance between hard, tangible resources and the intangible assets represented in talent and knowledge.

And so, Joe became the first CEO to enroll in the University of Pennsylvania's doctorate program in workplace learning leadership, alongside CLOs and other learning executives from many of the world's great companies. As he worked toward earning his doctorate, Joe built upon his earlier awareness of the importance of teaching and developing leaders and talent at all levels. In his doctoral program, Joe was exposed to new and additional ideas about the value that leaders serving as teachers can have on an organization. The leaders-as-teachers concept quickly became even more important and personal for him.

Signature Healthcare was investing 4 percent of its operating budget in training programs, but wasn't seeing the investment return on the level of performance improvements he and his board of directors were expecting. He knew that organizational learning would be essential, especially in light of significant changes introduced by the Affordable Care Act, to keep pace with change in the healthcare industry.

Penn's CLO Program illustrated for Joe what it takes to leverage learning and development to build new organizational capabilities. He realized that Signature's corporate learning team was essentially working in isolation and didn't have "enough exposure to the organization's needs" to adequately address the firm's growth strategies. He began to understand that leaders play an essential role in converting learning to performance by supporting their teams with coaching and opportunities to practice new skills as a follow-up to formal learning. But he wanted to further investigate the potential for leaders to have an even greater impact on performance if they were to be taught how to teach and facilitate.

Joe made the leaders-as-teachers concept the subject of his dissertation: "Application of Theories, Principles and Methods of Adult Learning for Managers to Improve Workplace Reactions to Learning, Knowledge, and Performance." The two questions at the center of his research were:

1. What is the general level of knowledge managers have about adult learning theories and facilitation methods?

2. If managers were trained to be great teachers, would their new competency affect hard business metrics such as earnings per share (EPS), profitability, return on investment (ROI), employee engagement scores from Gallup's Q12, and others that gauge business throughput?

Joe was determined to prove or disprove that an investment in developing leaders' teaching skills would pay off. He received unanimous approval from Signature's board of directors to pursue the study.

To conduct his research, Joe formed a test group of 15 managers to compare against his control group of 51 others. The research process began with a competency assessment of the managers' knowledge of both adult learning theories and the elements of what makes a great teacher. The test group then participated in a week-long program called the Healthcare Educator Series to learn about, and practice, teaching and facilitation skills.

The study followed performance indicators at all facilities for a period of nine months. Then, it examined the difference between the 15 facilities where test group managers served as the site's senior-most leaders, and the 51 remaining sites with senior leaders who had not attended the program. During this time, both test and control group managers had been asked to instruct and inform their teams on two important programs.

All of this enabled Joe to collect performance data on the firm, as well as Kirkpatrick assessment data on the two instructional programs that managers taught.

As a result, Joe amassed 35,000 pieces of data, making his research one of the largest quantitative studies ever conducted on the leaders-as-teachers concept.

"We had great findings that really showcased a couple things that are important," said Joe in a YouTube presentation of his results. "If a manager became a great teacher, their engagement scores from direct reports were much higher. We realized that when a manager could teach something like an initiative, a strategy, or a program for the company, it changed the relationship between them and the stakeholder base they work with."

The research further showed that employee turnover was lower in work locations where leader-teachers were present. "It showed that leaders-as-teachers does get returns that will excite your board and your C-suite," Joe proclaims.

While the evidence was convincing, Joe had long been confident that he would become an effective leader-teacher. Every two months, he hosts a two-day session with senior leaders, where he routinely takes a position at the head of the class to lead a dialog on issues that might impact the company's balanced scorecard metrics. He conducts sessions on how to predict, forecast, and prepare for the future.

Joe launched and teaches in Signature Healthcare's CEO School. The program has been delivered to more than 120 senior leaders, and Joe is a mainstay on the faculty, along with the company's chief financial officer (CFO), chief operating officer (COO), and other executives who share the teaching role.

The program includes roundtable discussions on how to revolutionize the long-term care industry, what's required to develop average performers into "A" players, how to master an "elevator speech" as a key CEO competency, and other topics that strengthen each leader's arsenal of skills.

The leaders-as-teachers concept continues to blossom. Signature's chief nursing officer conducts a directors of nursing program, in which Joe and other leaders teach assigned modules. For urgent issues and "hot topics," Joe and other leaders often teach virtual classes using web technology.

In onboarding programs for new employees, Signature Healthcare leaders teach the mission, vision, values, and metrics the company deems important in order to track performance. They also share their views on what sets Signature Healthcare apart in the long-term care industry.

As a CEO, Joe undoubtedly confronts a demanding daily workload that many senior leaders say leaves no time for teaching. But the formal programs described above don't even represent the sum of Joe's contribution as a leader-teacher. During a holiday break in 2010, he wrote a 43-page report summarizing and sharing his commentary on the book, *The 100 Best Business Books of All Time*. He shared how messages in many of the books shaped his own leadership philosophy, and offered inspiring messages, explanations, and words of encouragement to his leadership team throughout the paper.

And his leader-teacher activity list still is not done. Joe produces videotaped lectures, teaching on concepts like innovation, how to get jobs in healthcare, and the opportunities he expects to come from the Affordable Care Act. He regularly posts informative articles on his blog, www.JoeSteier.com. And finally, Joe wrote a book, *My God! Our God?* about his own very personal spiritual journey, and how his spirituality influences his role as a corporate leader.

Joe said in one video lecture that a few decades ago employees were told to do their jobs and "just don't mess anything up." He found that work, under those conditions, was boring. He encourages people to tell their employers what they "want to do," to "share their boldest ideas," and to "show their hearts" in their work. He describes how the American spirit is fueling entrepreneurs who are, right now, driving many breakthroughs to address and solve the healthcare changes the United States is facing.

Perhaps it makes sense to extend his leader-teacher role with these further distinctions: leader-motivator, leader-instigator, leader-cheerleader, and simply, Leader (with a capital L).

Glossary

Active teaching: In contrast to teaching primarily through the use of lectures and formal presentation of PowerPoint decks, active teaching involves a variety of methods that engages participants in a more experiential way. Such teaching typically increases involvement, learning, and levels of retention.

Co-leaders: Organizations frequently deploy leader-teachers in pairs, trios, or small teams to teach a program. Program champions sometimes consist of two or possibly three individuals. Each of these combinations are examples of leader-teacher co-leadership.

Go to the light: The change strategy of making progress by finding the energy in the organization and tapping into it. For leaders-as-teachers, this means finding individuals and organizational pockets with interest, enthusiasm, and willingness to dedicate resources to using the LAT approach. Experience shows that once people "see the light," more people and departments will embrace and share it.

Guided learning journey (GLJ): This is a method of social collaborative learning with a wide variety of uses. It is characterized by its perspective that the learning journey never ends, but continues into the workplace. The traditional teacher is replaced by faculty who support the learning process. This method typically spans several weeks rather than day-long sessions.

Guiding coalition: This is a term coined by John Kotter. It is an essential part of a successful change management process. A guiding coalition usually consists of two or more individuals who drive a successful change initiative.

Leaders-as-teachers (LAT) approach: The process by which an organization mobilizes its leaders to teach in learning programs and informally, using just-in-time teaching moments and opportunities.

Leader-teacher: A person who is a functional, team, or business leader and who has taken on the role of being part of a learning program, most commonly as a facilitator or trainer, but sometimes as a training designer, advisor, or reviewer. A leader can also serve as teacher and coach in a less programmatic fashion. This informal teaching usually occurs in-the-moment by taking advantage of the many daily opportunities to help others learn, grow, and change for the better.

Learning gems: This is a teaching method that encourages learners to individually or collectively reflect on their most important learning and ideas for application of their respective learning. Learning gems can be identified through a variety of methods, including collecting learning gems on post-it notes, flip charts, "Ah Ha" sheets, and so on.

Learning management system (LMS): A software application for the administration, documentation, tracking, and reporting of training programs and learning activities and events. A LMS is typically associated with and includes e-learning delivery.

Program champion: A program champion is a leader-teacher who is the designated leader of a program. The program champion usually works with a learning and development professional to assure excellence in program design, business alignment, continuous program improvement, and ready availability of highly qualified leader-teacher faculty for the program.

Progression: A progression is a plan used to enable leaders to assume increasingly challenging teaching assignments and build their teaching comfort level. Each progression should stretch the leaders as they build new skills.

Silos/silo busting: Silos is a term used to describe highly insular, compartmentalized, or vertical organizational behavior. Using leader-teachers with multi-business and multi-functional groups is a way to break down silo-like behavior and thinking. When implemented successfully, a leader-teacher approach can have a positive silo-busting impact on an organization.

Unique leadership perspective (ULP): A ULP reflects the essence of what a leader believes, acts upon, models, teaches, and expects of herself and others in the organization. While ULPs are apparent in leaders' day-to-day actions, decisions, and communications, ULPs often come to life in the form of stories, anecdotes, and career reflections that have a personal and authentic feel.

References

"2011 Top Companies for Leaders, Survey Highlights." (2012). Aon Hewitt.

Berrett, D. (2012). "How 'Flipping' the Classroom Can Improve the Traditional Lecture." *The Chronicle of Higher Education,* February 19. Accessed at: http://chronicle.com/article/How-Flipping-the-Classroom/130857.

Betof, E. (2009). *Leaders as Teachers. Unlocking the Teaching Potential of Your Company's Best and Brightest.* Alexandria, VA: ASTD Press.

Betof, E. and L.M.D. Owens. (2013). "Results of a 2013 Leaders as Teachers Study Among Conference Board Councils." Unpublished research report.

Betof, E. and N. Betof. (2010). *Just Promoted! A 12-Month Road Map for Success in Your New Leadership Role.* 2nd edition. New York: McGraw-Hill.

Bloom, B.S. and G. Madaus. (1981). *Evaluation to Improve Learning.* New York: McGraw-Hill.

Boroditsky, K. (2010). "Lost in Translation." *The Wall Street Journal.* July 23.

Brinkerhoff, R.O. (2003). *The Success Case Method: Find Out Quickly What's Working and What's Not.* San Francisco: Berrett-Koehler Publishers.

Collins, J. (2011). *Great by Choice: Uncertainty, Chaos, and Luck—Why Some Thrive Despite Them All.* New York: HarperCollins.

Collins, J. and M. Hansen. (2001). *Good to Great: Why Some Companies Make the Leap . . . and Others Don't.* New York: HarperCollins.

Fulmer, R. and B. Hanson. (2010). "Developing Leaders in High-Tech Firms—What's Different and What Works." *People & Strategy, September 1.*

Gawande, A. (2010). *The Checklist Manifesto: How to Get Things Right.* New York: Picador.

Gladwell, M. (2005). *Blink: The Power of Thinking Without Thinking.* New York: Little, Brown and Company.

Hamdan, N., P. McKnight, K. McKnight, and K. Arfstrom. (2013). "A Review of Flipped Learning." Flipped Learning Network. Accessed at: http://researchnetwork.pearson.com/wp-content/uploads/LitReview_FlippedLearning1.pdf.

Herrmann, K., A. Komm, J. McPherson, M. Lambsdorff, and S. Kelner. (2011). "Return on Leadership: Competencies that Generate Growth." McKinsey & Company and Egon Zehnder International.

Holland, S. (2012). "The Leadership Premium: How Companies Win the Confidence of Investors." Deloitte.

Jensen, E. (2000). *Brain-Based Learning: The New Science of Teaching and Training.* Seven Oakes, CA: Corwin.

Keysers, C. (2011). *The Empathic Brain.* Kindle Edition.

Klein, K.E. (2008). "A Practical Guide to Branding." *Bloomberg Business Week.* June.

Kotter, J.P. (2012). *Leading Change.* Boston: Harvard Business Review Press.

Kotter, J.P. and D.S. Cohen. (2012). *The Heart of Change: Real-Life Stories of How People Change Their Organizations.* Boston: Harvard Business Review Press.

Kouzes, J.M., B.Z. Posner. (2012). *The Leadership Challenge: How to Make Extraordinary Things Happen in Organizations.* 5th ed. San Francisco: Jossey-Bass.

Lafley, A.G., R. Martin, and J. Riel. (2013). "A Playbook For Strategy: The Five Essential Questions at the Heart of Any Winning Strategy." *Rotman Magazine,* Winter.

Mager, R.F. (1997). *Developing Attitude Toward Learning.* 2nd ed. Center for Effective Performance.

Martinuzzi, B. (2009). *The Leader as a Mensch: Become the Kind of Person Others Want to Follow.* San Francisco: Six Seconds Emotional Intelligence Press.

Medina, J. (2010). *Brain Rules: 12 Principles for Surviving and Thriving at Work, Home, and School.* Seattle: Pear Press.

Moore, D.M. and F.M. Dwyer. (1994). V*isual Literacy—A Spectrum of Visual Learning.* Englewood Cliffs, NJ: Educational Technology Publications.

Morrison, G.R., S.M. Ross, H.K. Kalman, and J.E. Kemp. (2011). *Designing Effective Instruction.* 6th ed. Indianapolis, IN: John C. Wiley & Sons.

"Mr. Clean." (2014). Wikipedia. Accessed at: http://en.wikipedia.org/wiki/Mr._Clean.

Nanovakovic, K. (2013). "Mirror-Data and Meta-Neurons." *Kristina Novakovic* (blog), May 13. Accessed at: http://kristinanovakovic.wordpress.com/2013/05/13/mirror-data-and-meta-neurons.

Owens, L.M.D. (2011). "Recall and Active Learning." Greater Cincinnati Chapter ASTD. http://www.gc.astd.org/Resources/Documents/Articles/activities_and_recall-lowens.pdf.

Ratkiewicz, K.S. and A.K. Wiete. (2010). *Leaders Developing Leaders: Capitalizing on the Demographic Gift to Revive Your Leadership Program.* The Human Capital Institute and Lee Hecht Harrison.

Ray, R. and D. Dearmond. (2013). "The DNA of Leaders: Leadership Development Secrets." Research Report R-1530-13-RR. The Conference Board.

Ringleb, A.H. and D. Rock (2008). "The Emerging Field of Neuroleadership." *NeuroLeadership Journal.*

Robb, S. (2013). " The 116 billion dollar brand question: what does Apple stand for?" Brand Lateral (blog), March 4. Accessed at: http://brand-lateral.com/2013/03/04/the-116-billion-dollar-brand-question-what-does-apple-stand-for.

Roberts, K. (2004). "On Screen - On Line - In Store." SaatachiKevin.com, June 18, Accessed at: www.saatchikevin.com/On_Screen_On_Line_In_Store.

Rock, D. (2008). "SCARF: A Brain-Based Model for Collaborating With And Influencing Others." *NeuroLeadership Journal.*

Romiszowski, A.J. (2004). "How's the E-learning Baby? Factors Leading to Success or Failure of an Educational Technology Innovation." *Educational Technology* 44(1): 5-27.

Sagger, R. (2009). "The Efficacy of Manager Teaching to Enhance Leadership Learning and Effectiveness." Ph.D. diss., McGill University.

Schoemer, K. (2009). *Change Is Your Competitive Advantage: Strategies for Adapting, Transforming, and Succeeding in the New Business Reality.* Amvon, MA: F+W Media.

Steier, J. (2010). "Application of Theories, Principles and Methods of Adult Learning for Managers to Improve Workplace Reactions to Learning, Knowledge and Performance." Ph.D. diss., University of Pennsylvania.

Stolovitch, H.D. and E.J. Keeps. (2011). *Telling Ain't Training.* 2nd ed. Alexandria, VA: ASTD Press.

Thiagarajan, S. (2006). *Thiagi's Interactive Lectures.* Alexandria, VA: ASTD Press.

Tufan, D. (2010). "E-Learning Completion and Dropout: Factors and Findings of Practice Aiming to Increase Participation in E-Learning in Corporate Environments." *3rd International Future-Learning Conference on Innovations in Learning for the Future 2010: e-Learning.* Retrieved from Academia.edu, September 10, 2013.

Index